January Bible Study

Psalms:
SONGS
FROM LIFE

Fred M. Wood

Convention Press • Nashville, Tennessee

Contents

This book is the text for a course in the subject area Bible Study of the Church Study Course.

Target group: This book is designed for adults and is part of the Church Study Course offerings. The 1963 statement of "The Baptist Faith and Message" is the doctrinal guideline for the writer and editor.

Dewey Decimal Classification Number: 223.2
Subject Heading: Bible O. T. Psalms
Printed in the United States of America.

A Word to Begin . . .

The Book of Psalms has been called humanity's hymnbook. Through the centuries, devout worshipers of God and interested seekers have identified with the psalmists' songs from life. The psalmists' humanness, honesty, and faith have touched responsive chords in countless lives.

The songs in humanity's hymnbook contain life's varied melodies: praise, thanksgiving, petition, lament, perplexity, anger, faith, vindictiveness, questioning. The whole range of human emotions is presented. Because the psalmists wrote in response to life's experiences and to God's leading, people today can draw strength and encouragement from their words.

Fred M. Wood, pastor of Eudora Baptist Church in Memphis, Tennessee, for thirty-one years and now engaged in a full-time preaching-teaching-writing ministry, wrote this textbook. He has given excellent treatment to selected psalms which represent the various kinds of psalms in the Psalter. Space limitations would not permit studying each psalm, or even treating all of the representative psalms that the Bible student would like to see presented. Perhaps, studying a limited number of psalms will motivate personal study of more of the songs from life.

To get the most out of your study of Psalms—and to make maximum use of this textbook—use a simple but helpful procedure. First, read the psalm that has been selected for detailed or summary study. Read from your Bible, and use more than one translation if you can do so. Then, with an open Bible, read the January Bible Study textbook. This method will make your study easier and more meaningful.

The textbook may be used in personal or group study. In both uses, the Personal Learning Activities at the end of each chapter will help the learner to review the material that has been covered. In group study, the companion Study Guide will provide helpful resources for the teacher and the members. The Teaching Guide which is contained in the *Psalms: Songs from Life Teaching Resource Kit, 1985*, will aid the teacher in directing the study. In this textbook, guidance for using Personal Learning Activities is in the section entitled "The Church Study Course" at the end of the book.

3

Also at the back of the book is a Church Study Course Credit request (Form 725). On completion of this book, the pupil should mail in the completed form to the address that is indicated. Twice each year, up-to-date reports called "transcripts" will be sent to churches to distribute to members who take part in the Church Study Course.

Eli Landrum, Jr., editor

1 Songs of Wisdom

To the Old Testament saint, wisdom was the greatest trait that one could possess. The person who refused to receive instruction resembled a fool who was rushing headlong to certain doom. So completely was this truth ingrained in Israel's life that a type of writing arose called Wisdom Literature. Some of the psalms fit in this category.

Although biblical writers sometimes saw wisdom as rooted in the fear (reverence) of the Lord, one should understand what they meant. They did not intend to portray a horrid, cringing dread of vengeance or a gloomy idea of deity as fate. Rather, they saw fear as a healthy reluctance to disobey a holy and wise God who wanted the highest good for all people. When in that God's favor, each person found life's true meaning.

By intelligent choices, the wise person developed quality and integrity in conduct. Psalms 1; 73; 112; 127 were chosen for this particular study because they reflect a life which was opened to a wider region of ethical power than one person ever could enjoy when restricted by legal codes. In many ways, these songs revealed the high-water mark of Old Testament thought.

The Wisdom Psalms center around two major emphases: (1) How does God deal with people who sin? (2) What is the relationship between virtue and reward? As the psalmists grappled with these two problems, they dealt with the burning issues of their day. Often, the truly good people in Israel found the going hard. Many secular-minded people lived in the comfort of material security; often, they almost made invalid the claims of religion by causing the righteous persons to feel that the good life was futile. The triumphant Wisdom Psalms rendered a great service to the nation. The people sang them constantly and rejoiced in the confidence that the songs brought to their sometimes discouraged lives.

The Way of Life and the Way of Death (1:1-6)

A Threshold Psalm

Psalm 1, the song of life's two ways, serves as an ideal preface to the entire collection of Hebrew songs. In only a few sentences, the psalmist expressed the substance of the complete volume and stated the great principle which runs through the entire book. Every known Bible version assigns first place to this Psalm which stresses the importance of obeying God's will and of trusting in his providential rule.

The psalmist expressed truths that could refer to any person on any occasion. The absence of a title adds to the broad scope of the Psalm's message and indicates its introductory nature.

The Happiness of the Righteous (vv. 1-3)

In verses 1-3, the psalmist painted with broad strokes a three-fold portrait of the good man. The word rendered **blessed** (v. 1) meant *happy*. The psalmist used the plural form to intensify his thought and to make it almost an exclamation. Some interpreters have translated the word as "Oh, the happinesses of" in an effort to catch the phrase's enthusiasm. The words expressed deep emotion in the form of poetic language.

In verse 1, the threefold picture of the righteous person begins with a negative description: what is absent from such a life. Three phrases, each of which has a threefold division, comprise the picture. Each set of three words shows a movement downward. The words "walks," "stands," and "sits" show a gradual moving toward a habitual style of living. The terse and simple terms describe powerfully the successive steps in an evil career; the last word forms the climax. First, the unrighteous person adopts the principles of wickedness as a rule for life; then, he persists in following the practices of notorious offenders; and finally, he becomes fixed in his evil ways.

The terms "counsel," "way," and "seat" also form a trio of deterioration. The righteous person does not listen to the advice of those who might serve as wrong counselors. Thus, he is not guided by these evildoers. This means that the good person refuses to conform to the example of sinners and to settle down with them to a fixed life-style. Finally, such a one never would sit in their meetings and take part in mocking sacred things.

The final set of three—"wicked," "sinners," and "scoffers"—

refers to the evil people whom the good person avoids. The terms also are listed in the order of their downward sequence. The word rendered "wicked" embraces all kinds and degrees of wrongdoing. It denotes misconduct in general; it does not call attention to specific sins or activated depravity such as the two terms that follow.

The second word, **sinners,** literally meant *those who miss the mark.* From this meaning came the idea of leaving the path of duty. Old Testament writers used the term for those who failed in the great goals of life by violating positive and known obligations.

The "scoffers" or scornful fell prey to evil's seductive power; and, in an effort to defend themselves, they openly mocked God. In blind arrogance, they tried to put themselves above God while they voiced their contempt for the things that ought to have been their foundation and support. This group represented the final result of lives which ignored God.

In verse 2, the psalmist described the righteous person by two positive qualities; both were related to the Lord's revealed will. The people of the psalmist's day understood the term **law** in several senses. Literally, the term meant *teaching, instruction,* or *direction.* From that meaning came the idea of a command. The Hebrews applied the word to the Pentateuch (the first five books of the Old Testament) or law of Moses; but as time passed, the term took on a broader meaning. It referred to all of the Old Testament books, since they were an exposition and application of the Law. Still later, the word came to have an even larger meaning: all the written revelation of God's will as far as people knew and understood it. The psalmist contended that the righteous person did not look on the Law as an irksome burden but as a joyful guide. The Law served as an unerring compass to regulate conduct and to produce a strong bond of trust in God's providential rule over every area of one's life.

The psalmist saw the Law as a source of constant inspiration as a person thought about it constantly and based daily decisions on it. The word translated **meditate** literally meant *to murmur* or *to mutter.* From this meaning came the idea of speaking in a low voice as one did when he or she considered a subject carefully. The righteous person attempted to understand the Law's meaning by reflecting—concentrating—on it. This individual kept the Law before his mind and had pleasure and satisfaction in this duty. He considered meditating on the Law to be a privilege. The phrase "day and night" expressed the fullness of time. It conveyed the thought that the good person exercised such mental discipline that meditating on the Law became a habit. When one did this regularly, the result was a refreshed spirit because thinking about divine truth brought one nearer to the eternal realities that come from fellowship with God. Even in the leisure hours, God's will pervaded the righteous person's whole being until it became his second nature; it filled life and laid claim to the whole person and to total conduct.

Verse 3 shows that such a righteous life produces positive results. In the hot Oriental countries, where heat and drought burn up the vegetation, trees flourish near watercourses. The phrase translated **streams of water** means *the division of the river where the ground is most fertile.* The term could denote a man-made canal or a natural stream. The Psalm also asserts that the righteous man is set in the place by God rather than accidentally finding himself in that location.

The green tree, full of sap and vigor, never lacks nourishment or fails to bring forth produce. Even the tree's appearance corresponds to the fruit. The leaves' refusing to dry up presents a striking image of a happy person.

The psalmist moved from a general statement to a concrete one. The godly person literally would cause to prosper all things that he attempted (v. 3). This meant that the righteous people would make progress. Today, sometimes one may not see instant success; the path may seem dark. However, success will come to the one who remains faithful. God will provide internal resources that will enable the person to triumph.

The Way of the Unrighteous (vv. 4-5)

The wicked individuals were set in sharp contrast to the righteous persons. The psalmist pictured the evil people as without value or meaning. He began his description with a simple phrase which literally reads: not so, the wicked. Nothing that was written about the good person was true of the evil one.

During harvesttime, the farmers spread the sheaves out on the threshing floor, usually in an elevated and exposed place outside the village. Then, they tossed the mixture into the air; as it was falling, the wind scattered the chaff. The psalmist compared the one who lived apart from God with the worthless chaff. The ungodly person lacked stability because he had no

substance and, therefore, did not endure.

Two lessons emerge clearly from the figure of speech "like chaff which the wind drives away" (v. 4). (1) The ungodly person's worthless life forfeits all semblance of security. Whether the term "judgment" (v. 5) stands for the final verdict at the end of the world or refers to the various crises of the present life, the conclusion is the same. Because the unrighteous person is rootless and fruitless, his/her ultimate fate is complete futility. (2) Whenever the fellowship of believers, the "congregation of the righteous" (v. 5), assembles—whether on earth or in the world to come—godly people comprise it. Therefore, the wicked persons find no place in such surroundings. They never feel comfortable, and they do not enjoy assembling with the righteous.

The Fate of Each (v. 6)

God understands people's true characters. This guards against the righteous people and the wicked individuals coming together improperly or being recompensed equally. The Lord approves only those who follow him in sincerity, and no one can impose on him by pretending to be righteous. He admits to his favor only those who deserve such reward and whose characters bear the searching gaze of divine inspection.

Humans may make mistakes in judging character, but God always judges properly. The word rendered "knows" indicates God's care for, approval of, and interest in the righteous person; the necessary results are blessings and rewards. Scripture writers often used this same word to express the marriage relationship. Therefore, the psalmist suggested that God loves and thus deals mercifully as he relates to the righteous individuals.

People who reflect God's tenderness in their lives have enormous influence for good. John Greenleaf Whittier expressed this truth beautifully in his poem "The Friend's Burial":

> The dear Lord's best interpreters
> Are humble, human souls;
> The Gospel of a life like hers
> Is more than books or scrolls.
>
> From scheme and creed the light goes out,
> This saintly fact survives;
> The blessed Master none can doubt
> Revealed in holy lives.

God also knows the folly of the ungodly persons and makes certain that wicked people with all of their pomp, pride, and worldly power will face ruin at the end. Evil living brings destruction, and one who lives a wicked life will not prosper in the end. The word translated "perish" first of all suggests lostness; but from this meaning come the ideas of destruction, the abyss, and complete nothingness.

From Doubt to Faith (73:1-28)

Verdict from Experience (v. 1)

The psalmist opened Psalm 73 with the conclusion at which he had arrived in his soul's struggle. He couched the message in the form of a flashback that gave the process by which he had come to his judgment.

The word rendered **pure** means *clean* and refers to those who hold to their integrity in spite of all circumstances that test their loyalty to God. Although the Lord sometimes delays his vindication of the good, the righteous person receives a proper reward when God feels that the right time has come. The word translated "heart" refers to a person's total life, the seat of one's intelligence and will. God responds with good acts and gifts to those whose lives are clean.

The Psalmist's Problem (vv. 2-3)

The psalmist passed through some bad days and almost fell victim to pessimism. Cynicism threatened as he thought about the situation that existed. He came close to losing his faith as he looked at people's conduct. He saw evil persons receive good things though they defied God's moral law. He became jealous when he saw those who spoke with proud words succeed in life. He nearly lost confidence in God as a wise and just, moral governor. The psalmist knew that God decided everyone's ultimate fate; but as he viewed the land, he began to doubt that God really controlled things. The religious leaders taught that wicked people were not content, but the psalmist saw the evil individuals enjoying perfect peace.

The word translated **prosperity** (v. 3) is the Hebrew word *shalom* which is used even today for *peace*. It means more than the absence of conflict. A person at peace is one who is emotionally whole and well adjusted in his/her entire personality. Peace is total well-being under God's rule. To the psalmist, the evil people about him attained this goal when they should have been suffering because of their sins.

Picture of the Wicked (vv. 4-9)

The psalmist already had described the wicked persons as arrogant; they were proud almost to the point of madness. Then, he pictured these evil people in detail. For one thing, they went to the grave with no torment. The word **pangs** (v. 4) meant *tightly drawn cords* as though one were twisted or tortured. The psalmist saw that as the wicked died, they did not suffer in proportion to their wickedness. The seeming lack of any divine displeasure with them caused him to be uneasy. He contended that they should have gone to the grave in great agony because they had enjoyed the sinful things of the world. He felt that God seemed to show a special interest in them. The Lord even seemed to save them from life's common calamities (v. 5).

Although the psalmist used two figures of speech in verse 6, the wicked literally may have put on ornaments and trappings which reflected their conceit. They may have adorned their clothing with things which showed that they thought highly of themselves. Also, since injustice and cruelty formed such a part of their lives, their clothing may have resembled and showed their greed and force.

Tension gripped the psalmist as he saw wicked people indulge in unholy living but not become weak and drawn by toil and want. He felt that those who indulged in worldly things should suffer, but their fat faces (v. 7) indicated their prosperity. The statement, "Their hearts overflow with follies" (v. 7), indicated that their plans moved along without any problems. They got almost everything they wished for, and they suffered no penalty for their sins.

The wicked lived in ease and enjoyment; they attached to themselves an inflated importance which caused them to speak with scorn against everyone, including God (vv. 8-9). The psalmist described their perverse behavior by their speech. They issued proud commands that were full of reproach and bitterness against God, and they used the entire earth as their theater. They tried to clothe themselves with all power as though they were superior beings with a right to command. The wicked people showed no regard for authority and set themselves above all law as though no one in heaven or earth had any right to control them.

Effect on the People (vv. 10-11)

The psalmist noted how easily wicked people corrupted the masses. He saw how many individuals were drawn to copy the wicked persons' evil examples and even to adopt their speech patterns. The people drank in the wicked individuals' words and expressions and adopted their sarcastic approaches.

Some scholars have felt that verses 10-11 represented words of those who truly loved God. The words pictured the faithful people as returning in their musings to the subject of the wicked persons' prosperity; they were perplexed by the evil individuals' success. The righteous people thought about it and became more perplexed and embarrassed. They could not solve the problems that the facts suggested about the wicked individuals. Translations vary, but one thing is certain: The psalmist felt unable to cope with the problem that the success of those who defied God raised.

The Psalmist's Reflection (vv. 12-14)

After the psalmist related the wicked persons' harmful effect on others, he recorded his reaction to their freedom from trouble. He felt that they were protected from calamity, and he made their success more vivid by contrasting it to his frustration. He knew that he had kept his life clean (v. 13) and had lived free from the terrible iniquity of those whom he had observed. He had fulfilled the ritualistic washing of his hands as the Law required and had done so in sincerity, not as a cover-up for a tainted life (v. 13). The psalmist felt that he had every reason to expect God's blessings, but instead severe physical suffering came to him which lasted the whole day and even broke out afresh the next day (v. 14). If he had doubted the wicked people's characters he might accept matters with a better frame of mind. However, he knew that their wickedness was an open record. Yet, they experienced no reverses but went through life tranquil, happy, and successful.

The Doubter's Dilemma (vv. 15-16)

A thought plagued the psalmist: Should he express his feelings publicly? One may assume that he was influential in the religious community and that his opinions carried weight because the people esteemed him. However, he knew that if he uttered all that was in his mind, he would hurt other people (v. 15). He did not wish to undermine the faith of someone weaker and less able to cope with the problem. He concluded that those who feared God should trust him and never should let their inward doubts become public.

Verse 16 summarizes the psalmist's attempt to weigh all the facts. The word **thought** means *to ponder* and suggests that the psalmist kept on pondering in an effort to reach a conclusion which would satisfy him. He tried to explain it to himself, but the more he rolled it over in his mind, the more the problem grew. The Hebrew word rendered "wearisome" suggests labor, toil, or burden. He viewed the question as too weighty for his weak powers.

Answers Through Worship (v. 17)

The skeptic discovered what many honest doubters have learned: Prayer and worship change one's viewpoint! The word **sanctuary** meant *a place of worship*. It came from a word that meant *to be holy*, but the literal meaning was *something set* *apart*. The psalmist may have referred to the Temple or to the tabernacle. He meant that he went to a quiet place that was apart from the busy world where he could meditate and meet God for instruction.

Of course, formal worship brings a unique blessing. When we gather as a fellowship of believers, strength comes; we go away with renewed dedication and deeper insight.

One Sunday during my seminary days, I stayed home from my church field because of snow and ice. I studied on Saturday and attended church with my wife and small baby on Sunday morning. Late that afternoon, I faced a decision about Sunday night. Should I walk about a mile to the nearby church (my car was at my church field) or stay home? After all, I would be in class on Monday morning studying the Bible. Did I need church that night? I went to church, and I still remember the message that Rollins Burhan preached. Although the incident took place nearly forty years ago, I still remember how happy I was as I walked away from that service where I had worshiped with fellow believers.

However, collective worship must be balanced by individual worship. Nothing takes the place of a time alone with the Lord, thinking about him and seeking to understand his purposes and his leadership. When the psalmist worshiped God, he saw new truths and saw that the Lord still controlled the world and the people in it.

Fate of the Wicked (vv. 18-20)

The psalmist took a fresh start and used the same word with which he began his poem (v. 18). Light dawned on him, and in the darkness of his conflict God opened his eyes to the evil-doers' certain destiny. He saw that the Lord had placed them where they had no firm foundation but easily would lose their footing and slide into confusion and desolation. The word translated "dost set them" (v. 18) indicated continuous action, while the phrase "make them fall" suggested completed action as though God already had determined that the event would take place. God went on setting them in slippery places; their fall was certain.

The psalmist's exclamation stressed the uncertainty, the danger, and the sudden ruin that would overtake the wicked people (v. 19). The calamities reversed the wicked persons' apparent prosperity. The horrible fate which awaited them proved that their outward appearance of prosperity was not their final lot.

Even during their prosperous period, they stood exposed to God's judgment.

The psalmist compared the evildoer's apparently good fortune with what one imagined to be true but suddenly learned was only a fantasy. Reality set in when the night's reverie passed and the morning light appeared. When this occurred, one resented the image that floated before his imagination. Every false conception vanished, and the wicked persons were left alone with their works which they learned to hate because the works brought them only misery.

Change of Attitude (vv. 21-22)

The psalmist admitted his former error and attributed it to his worried state of mind. The term **embittered** (v. 21) came from a word which meant *to be sour* or *leavened*. Of course, it referred to the fermenting process in making bread. The term **pricked** came from a word that meant *to sharpen*. Both words indicated that the psalmist had stirred himself up with his strong feelings on the subject. The word rendered "soul" usually was translated *heart* which stood for the rational part of one's personality. The word translated "heart" (v. 21) referred to the body's inward or secret parts, the reins or kidneys. Thus, the psalmist pictured how he was disturbed both in his thought process and in his emotions. He thought bad thoughts, and he felt bad feelings. His bad thoughts and feelings caused a sharp sword to penetrate his life.

The psalmist realized that his self-esteem had hit rock bottom. He had acted stupidly, like one who was controlled by emotions and not by reason (v. 22). As his mind reverted to his distress, he saw how dull he had been. He had acted more like a dumb animal than a thinking human being. The way that the psalmist introduced verse 22 emphasized how completely he blamed himself for his stupidity. Literally, the words read: I, even I, was stupid. He had no defense for his irritable and pevish action.

Return of Faith (vv. 23-26)

The psalmist felt himself once more to be a member of the worshiping community. He realized that God had not abandoned him in his affliction. The phrase "hold my right hand" (v. 23) meant that God would not allow the fellowship to be broken even though sometimes the psalmist could not see through the mystery of God's plan or understand his guidance.

God's grasp assured the psalmist that, at the proper time, the Lord would receive him in honor and vindicate him. In verse 24, the psalmist rose to one of the most profound statements in the entire Psalter. One Old Testament scholar wrote that the psalmist was "certain that a material event like the dissolution of the body . . . [was] powerless to break the love-forged links of the soul."[1] Another commented: "Such perfect communion with God manifestly could not brook the thought of its own cessation."[2] The psalmist desired nothing more than fellowship with God; any other wish faded into insignificance (v. 25). He knew that since God led him along the path of the present life, God would continue to be with him whatever the future held (v. 24).

Since the psalmist felt a need for God, he also was confident that nothing else could fill that divinely shaped vacuum (v. 25). The One who delivered him from his doubts and held him with a powerful grasp meant everything to him because this One provided the happiness of personal fellowship. All selfish impulses disappeared in the face of communion with God; this experience gave the psalmist strength to conquer every foe and to master even his suffering.

The psalmist concluded his testimony with a vivid contrast. He singled out the worst thing that could happen and indicated that even if such should arise, he joyfully could affirm his faith in God (v. 26). The psalmist came to a completely spiritual concept of religion. He desired the Lord exclusively and believed in God for God's own sake rather than merely for any reward that might come. The psalmist expressed his complete confidence in the power of faith in God to master life so completely that life on earth would survive every doubt. Even when the powers of the psalmist's mind and body were exhausted, God's love would survive and would provide strength and defense.

A Closing Contrast (vv. 27-28)

Psalm 73 closes with a summary of the great opposites. Those who reject life's primary fountain by refusing to respond to God fall prey to ruin. Verses 27-28 parallel the three with which the psalmist opened his song and gather up the double truth which he grasped more firmly because of his doubts. The riddles of life remained, but no one could deprive him any longer of his ultimate certainty that he found when he entered God's sanctuary. A life that was lived apart from the Lord would come to nothing, but one who sought constant fellowship with the Lord emerged victorious. In these closing words, one can feel an implicit appeal for loyalty at a time when the good people in the community who felt as the psalmist did were in danger of losing their faith.

The psalmist came out of his agitation and vexation with a desire to give his testimony (v. 28). In order to satisfy this impulse to tell of his inner spiritual struggle and victory, he linked himself with the most sacred relationship that he knew: fellowship with God. As he confided in the Lord and made God the sole ground of his reliance, the compulsion to share his faith with others grew. He learned that the one who took refuge in God developed courage to proclaim and to celebrate with gratitude the Lord's great works.

Reverence for God (112:1-10)

Psalm 112 deals with the good fortune of those who respect God and seek to serve him. The Psalm begins by enlarging on the thought in the last verse of Psalm 111. Some scholars suggest that the same person wrote both Psalms. In the former, the psalmist celebrated the Lord's power, goodness, and righteousness; in the latter, he described the prosperity, beneficence, and righteousness of those who respected and followed God.

Although Psalm 112 is arranged with an acrostic (alphabetic) style, the message is not a mere string of easy-to-remember sentences. The thoughts follow one another smoothly and with evident relatedness. Psalm 112 resembles Psalm 1 in subject matter but lays a stronger emphasis on the praise of godliness and gives less prominence to the wicked people. In simple terms, Psalm 112 begins with a general statement concerning the happiness of the one who sincerely reverences the Lord and finds joy in obeying his pronouncements (v. 1).

In the succeeding verses, the psalmist stated the advantages of a pious life. In verse 2, he called attention to the fact that such a person's posterity would prosper. In verse 3, he indicated the wealth that would come. In verse 4, the psalmist described the light which sprang up to dispel the darkness because the Lord is holy and compassionate. Verse 5 pointed out that the one who showed a liberal spirit in dealing with others and administered his own business with fairness prospered and found contentment. Verses 6-8 showed the firmness and composure of mind that such a person had in crises. Psalm 112 closed with a picture of the righteous man who was held in great esteem and rewarded by God, but who was envied by the wicked person who perished because of his pride and hostility (vv. 9-10).

The psalmist recognized clearly the Godlike character of a moral life and expressed it concisely and forcefully. Today, with the psalmist's printed insight, one can rejoice with the good persons as blessings flow into the life of the individual's family and his/her descendants. This strength stands out much more clearly when it is contrasted to the helpless anger of the envious, wicked person whose base ambitions are doomed to frustration and disappointment.

Unless the Lord Builds the House (127:1-5)

Psalm 127 clearly falls into two parts: verses 1-2 and verses

3-5. At first glance, these sections appear to be unrelated in subject matter. However, closer study reveals a dynamic connection. The Psalm expresses clearly the basic truth that human effort alone fails in life's most important efforts and issues. The examples that the Psalm presents deal with the home, the city, and the family. It contends that in these endeavors, God's leadership is the first essential to happiness and success.

Some scholars feel that David wrote Psalm 127 for his son Solomon as a guide for his life and his great building project, constructing the Temple. Others contend that Solomon wrote it as he anticipated building the house.

Psalm 127 majors on one subject: total dependence on God for success and the vanity of all efforts that the Lord does not bless. Verse 1 deals with the futility of building a house or of guarding a city without God. Verse 2 extends the thought to anxious concern about life's necessities and the work that must be done to provide for one's family.

The natural transition moved to the family as verses 3-5 stressed the truth that God sends children as a blessing. The psalmist held that one who possessed many children gained comfort and honor from them. God's approval and favor were/are the most important ingredients in a happy and successful life.

Lessons for Life from Psalms 1; 73; 112; 127

One who wishes to please God must study his Word.— Nothing takes the place of knowing what the Bible says about the main aspects of the Christian life. The Scriptures give assurance to a person who will learn their contents and follow their teachings. The Bible becomes a lamp to people's feet only when it is studied and made a part of life.

If honest doubting is dealt with wisely and sincerely, it can lead to a deeper faith.—However, those who wish to have such an experience must be honest with the facts and hold to their integrity. Formal worship helps to move one to understand more about God's nature, his purposes in the world, and the way he does his work.

Those who are truly righteous will be blessed in many ways.—Their families will honor them, and their neighbors will respect them. Their lives will have a stability that nothing else can give and nothing can take away. They will be fearless and fixed. God will honor them, and wicked people will be frustrated at the righteous persons' success in living lives of high quality.

Those who leave God out of their lives are doomed to failure.—Happiness depends on God's presence in every area of life. Homes, cities, and people's lives need to be based on godly principles. Regardless of how wise people are in worldly things, they will fail without the Lord.

---

1. W. O. E. Oesterley, *The Psalms* (London: Society for Promoting Christian Knowledge), II: 344.

2. Albert C. Knudson, *The Religious Teachings of the Old Testament* (New York: Abingdon-Cokesbury Press, 1918), p. 402.

Personal Learning Activities

1. Psalm 1 is a poem of (choose the correct answer from the list):
   ___(1) God's law   ___(3) The evil person
   ___(2) Life's two ways   ___(4) The fruitful tree
2. In Psalm 73, the psalmist's problem was _____. (Select the proper response from the list.)
   (1) Enemies' threats   (3) The prosperity of the wicked
   (2) His sin   (4) National crisis
3. In Psalm 112, the psalmist stated that no advantages came from living a pious life. True___ False___
4. Psalm 127 presents three examples to stress that God's leadership is essential to happiness and success. From the list, choose the correct answers.
   ___(1) The home   ___(4) The nation
   ___(2) The military   ___(5) The king
   ___(3) The city   ___(6) The family

Answers: 1. (2); 2. (3); 3. False; 4. (1), (3), (6).

2 Songs of Royalty

The Israelites gave their kings a unique place in national life. They held that these rulers had certain privileges and powers that were more than human. God mediated his blessings to the people through the kings. The date of a king's reign in Jerusalem was calculated from the first New Year's Day after his predecessor's death. The people viewed this special day as a time when God reaffirmed his covenant with the nation. Anointing the new king was a religious act and was performed by a priest or a prophet. High hopes arose for each new ruler who ascended the throne.

As the years passed, the messianic hope expressed itself in many forms. During the Mosaic Period, the people conceived of the coming Messiah as an ideal prophet. The people of Eli and Samuel's day looked for one who would perform the function of a priest. When David came to the throne, he captured the people's imagination so completely that for centuries they continued to look for someone like him to come and save the nation. During the Divided Kingdom following Solomon's death, the people often must have said: What we need in this country is another David!

This study deals with four psalms; two of them (2; 110) are connected directly with the ascension of God's anointed representative to the throne. The other two (20; 45) are concerned with matters that were related to the king's reign and personal life. In Psalm 20, the psalmist prayed that God would protect the king in order to assure military victory. Psalm 45 celebrated the king's marriage, perhaps to a foreign princess. New Testament writers referred directly to three of these Psalms (2; 45; 110).

21

The Ideal King (2:1-12)

Plot Against God's King (vv. 1-3)

When a mighty ruler died, any unrest that lay dormant immediately surfaced. Agitated people saw this as a time to lead an attack against the incoming monarch. Psalm 2 was written against the background of a new king's coming to the throne.

In verse 1, the psalmist wrote what he saw by a question which showed that he was amazed and angered as he viewed the attempt of Israel's foes to unseat the new king. The question was asked not so much to get an answer as to express surprise because the plot was futile. The psalmist was sure that the people who had set themselves against God's decree were doomed as hopelessly as stars that plotted to abolish the law of gravity. The word translated "conspire" suggested the idea of a bustling crowd or people running together as in a tumult. The word rendered **plot** meant *to murmur* or *to meditate* and was used for the growling of a lion over his prey. The enemies ran together and busily, noisily laid their plans.

In verse 2, both the words translated "set" and "take counsel" had the idea of firmness. The first was used for a conqueror who

22

sought to stand fixed while the second meant laying a building's foundation and thus settling or establishing it. The enemies set themselves in a fixed, firm position for battle. In Hebrew, the word "set" conveyed the thought that the rulers were seeking to do the work in their own strength. However, the psalmist contended that any action against the one whom God had chosen struck against God.

The word **anointed** literally meant *to draw the hand over anything*. The idea was that of smearing or rubbing over with oil. From this came the idea of consecrating or appointing. The term **messiah** came from this word and meant *one who had been set apart or anointed for a special service*.

Those who engaged in the plot looked on the Lord and his anointed as having the same purpose: to rule the world. The psalmist knew this and put words into the wicked kings' mouths. They wanted to break the power of God's ruler, but they planned to use their freedom for their interests rather than to advance the cause of justice in the world. They shouted encouraging words to each other and felt that they could reach their goal easily. God's restraints irked them, and they showed no patience; rather, they desired immediate release.

In verse 3, the word "bonds" symbolized the authority to which the wicked felt that the Lord's anointed subjected them. The figure of speech came from the fastenings by which the yoke was secured on oxen's necks. The word "cords" might have conveyed in another form the same idea as the term "bonds." Most likely, however, the word "cords" was a stronger word; the first term symbolized the yoke for plowing while the second meant the reins by which the animal was guided and kept under control. The entire picture indicated a state of mind that resented any discipline and desired complete self-expression to pursue personal ambitions.

The first stanza of Psalm 2 made such an impression on the people through the centuries that Peter and John, who did not have a formal education, quoted it in their prayer (Acts 4:25-26) to describe the plot against Jesus. The contrast that was present when God's power confronted people's proud attempts to overthrow him permeated the entire Psalm. Many scholars have viewed the first stanza as a prologue. They have held that it sets the stage by giving an impressive picture of the madness that seized the people and caused them to conspire against God's eternal purposes.

Divine Response to Rebels (vv. 4-6)

The psalmist turned from the wild tumult of battle and focused on God. He saw the divine reaction to the earthly rulers' arrogance. Above their defiance, he heard a voice thunder against the rebels. The One who was enthroned in majesty and glory, and who controlled all that took place on earth, would allow nothing to hinder the working of his will. God derided the boundless stupidity of those who thought that they could thwart his plans.

The parallel phrases in verse 4 are progressive. The verb **laugh** is milder; and though it does have a derived meaning *to make sport* or *to jest*, the basic idea is softer than the Hebrew term translated **has them in derision.** The second word basically means *to mock* or *to deride.* The bold figure of speech made vivid the truth that the world's sovereign Ruler surveyed the petty plottings with contempt. The psalmist contrasted the earth's helpless kings with the heavenly Ruler's superior might. He viewed the matter as a race of pygmies face-to-face with a giant! He knew that God's power surpassed all of his creatures' works. The psalmist expressed the truth graphically as he painted an exalted throne with the One seated on it smiling at the manikins (little people) below. In most Hebrew manuscripts, the word rendered **Lord** is the Hebrew term that conveys God's sovereignty. Since the psalmist was addressing the nations, he stressed the universal Ruler of the world rather than Israel's covenant God.

As verses 2-3 of the first stanza pictured the rebels speaking, verses 5-6 of the second stanza presented the Lord stating his case. God's irresistible will opposed the rebels' vain undertaking. He neither could remain unconcerned nor look calmly on their activities. The psalmist knew that God would not allow their schemes to succeed. The word "wrath" should not be understood to suggest unreasonable passion. Although God always controlled himself, he would act in a manner which was designed to show that the evil plotters could not succeed. Thus, he would restrain others from attempting a similar course of action. When the kings and rulers set themselves against God, he had no option. He had to exert his strength in order to reveal the impotence of those who opposed him. The psalmist saw God's laughter pass into the utterance of his wrath at the time that God felt was proper. Only God knew when long, drawn-out, gentle patience should end and opponents of righteousness should be crushed. When that time arrived, he would send forth his word of judgment.

The parallelism in verse 5 also is progressive. The words rendered "wrath" and "fury" come from different Hebrew terms; the word translated "fury" is much stronger. The word **wrath** comes from a word which means *to breathe through the nose* or *to snort;* becoming angry is a derived meaning. Thus, the resulting idea is "wrath." The second term comes from a word that means *to burn* or *to become hot;* thus, the idea is that of anger or "fury." Also, the words translated "speak" and "terrify" present a contrast. The one rendered "speak" is much milder than the one rendered "terrify." The latter suggests agitation and dismay, and also haste in executing one's action. The artistic way that verse 5 was written conveyed the idea of building to a climax. God would speak in wrath, and his wrath would build to a fury that would devastate the plotters.

The Lord's strong statement in verse 6 is in sharp contrast to the rebels' defiant words in verse 3. The sentence opens with strong emphasis on the word "I." Some versions have the word "yet" preceding this word, for the Hebrew text has a conjunction. One might insert the term "but" in order to catch the writer's exact thought: But I have set my king on Zion. The rebels had planned to cast off God's authority, but the psalmist knew that God could not allow them to prevent the Lord from establishing his chosen king. The word translated **set** came from a term that meant *to pour,* and from this came the idea *to pour out as in making a libation to God.* Thus, the derived meaning was to anoint a king. God had anointed his king "on Zion."

The psalmist wrote of Zion in both a poetical and functional sense when he referred to it as the anointed one's royal seat. This ancient stronghold was captured from the Jebusites and became the city of David. The ark of the covenant rested there until Solomon's temple was built. Old Testament writers used it as the symbolic name for Jerusalem; they considered it to be the Lord's dwelling place. Since this hill stood for the place where the divine Presence rested and spiritually excelled all of earth's other heights, the psalmist assigned to it the location of God's throne.

Originally, the word **holy** meant *separate* or *other than* but came to mean *set apart for a definite purpose.* As Hebrew religion developed, the word took on a moral and an ethical content. The latter meaning is intended in verse 6. Zion was a place that had been set apart.

Message from the King (vv. 7-9)

In verse 7, the psalmist introduced the one whom the Lord chose to rule. The ruler gave his defense to the throne. The king claimed that he was no usurper and that he had not assumed rule in order to gratify his ambition. The psalmist gave no transitional word or formal introduction from the Lord's speech in verse 6 to the king's words in verse 7. He merely stated what he saw and heard.

The first three Gospel writers applied the essence of the Lord's words in verse 7 to Jesus at his baptism. In Paul's sermon at Pisidian Antioch (Acts 13:33), he used the phrase once. The author of Hebrews used it twice, once to show Jesus' superiority to angels (Heb. 1:5) and the other to refer to the Savior's priesthood (Heb. 5:5). New Testament writers definitely saw the Messiah in Psalm 2.

Although sonship involved the privilege of inheritance as one of its natural rights, verse 8 stated clearly that the son had to ask for the promise and claim its fulfillment. God's design to set the king as his son included giving him a dominion that took in the uttermost part ("ends," v. 8) of the earth. In the psalmist's day, the Israelites divided the world into two parts: their own nation and all the other nations combined. They considered themselves to be God's people and all others to be heathen. This distinction still existed in New Testament days under the terms *Jew* and *Gentile*. God determined that his king's reign would embrace all nations, including those which at that time were not under the influence of true religion. He set no time for this to be realized, but he left no doubt that it would happen.

In verse 9, the Lord assigned absolute power to the king. The ruler was able to do more than to protect his friends. God gave him the ability to punish and to restrain his enemies.

The parallel statements in verse 9 are not exactly synonymous (the same idea expressed in different words) but rather almost antithetical (the second statement presenting a contrast to the first). The Hebrew word translated **break** is similar to another which means *to shepherd*. The Greek translation of the Old Testament, the Septuagint, renders it "thou shalt feed"; the Latin Vulgate translates "thou shalt rule," possibly as a compromise between the two ideas. If one takes the word to mean *to shepherd*, the "rod of iron" becomes a shepherd's staff; but still it is a symbol of stern and irresistible rule.

The next phrase in verse 9 symbolized complete and irreparable destruction. If the plotters proceeded with their scheme to overthrow the king, utter catastrophe would be their fate. Their confederacy would be shattered into fragments which could not be reunited.

Warning to the Plotters (vv. 10-12)

The psalmist had presented words from the rebels (vv. 1-3), the Lord (vv. 4-6), and the new king (vv. 7-9). He closed with his own words to those who felt that they could challenge God. The word "now" which introduced the stanza was not temporal (indicating the present) but argumentative. The statement could be phrased: Since things were so in God's world, the rebels should recognize reality. In the fourth stanza, the psalmist came back to his starting point. The train of thought which dominated the entire psalm, however, was that God stood behind his king and would oppose all who resisted his reign.

Verse 10 addressed two classes of people. The word translated **rulers** meant *judges, those who dispensed justice.* Both classes of national leaders—kings and judges—performed an important function and needed to recognize their limited power. The God of righteousness had all authority and had sufficient resources to discipline leaders.

In verse 10, the words "be warned" were a bit stronger than the words "be wise." The word that was directed to the kings first of all meant to act prudently. The form of the word that was used, however, meant to consider or to have understanding. The word that was directed to the judges was much stronger. The root idea was to chasten, to exhort, or to warn.

The psalmist concluded his ultimatum with a twofold command in order that the people might prevent the Lord's fury from breaking forth on them. In the Hebrew text, verse 11 contains two parallel statements. Literally, it reads: Serve the Lord with fear and rejoice with trembling. Once more, the psalmist used stronger words in the second phrase. The word **serve** basically meant *to work or labor* while a second word, which is present in the Hebrew but is omitted in the Revised Standard

Version, means to exult and also has in it the idea of to tremble. One could translate it, tremble with trembling.

The words "fear" and "trembling" follow the same pattern. The term **fear** is not nearly as strong as the word **trembling,** which comes from a term that means *to quake or shake with awe.* One might understand the second phrase to be the result of the first one, but more likely the writer meant the two phrases to be parallel commands to those who opposed the Lord's anointed.

Translators do not agree that the phrase "kiss his feet" (v. 12) renders the Hebrew text correctly. The Hebrew word translated **kiss** comes from an old Arabic term that means *to join* or *to arrange.* From this comes the idea in Hebrew of regulating or arming oneself and thus to kiss by joining mouth-to-mouth. The form of the Hebrew verb in verse 12 is rendered best "kiss" as in the Revised Standard Version. The word rendered **feet** comes from a Hebrew term which means *to create, form, or make.* From this comes the idea of a son or grandson. A derived meaning of the Hebrew word **son** is *a new or wonderful thing.* This could mean that the rebels were to give their homage or allegiance to this new king who had been placed on the throne. He was God's new and wonderful creation; therefore, he deserved their loyalty.

The psalmist left no doubt about how serious the rebels' choice was. The word rendered **perish** came from a term that meant *to stray or wander* and thus *to be lost.* From this, one could get the idea of being led into an abyss. The word rendered **quickly** came from a term which meant *to be or become little or few.* The idea could have been that the rebels virtually would be destroyed if God became angered only slightly. However, the word also could mean *a little while;* thus, it would convey the thought of *shortly* or *soon* and could be translated "quickly," probably the best rendering in the context of Psalm 2. This did not mean that God was impatient, but rather that he was capable of acting speedily to take vengeance on those who opposed his purposes.

The psalmist ended Psalm 2 on a joyful note. He congratulated those who put themselves under God's protecting hand. They would have their needs met and would have a relationship established that would enable them to face life without fear. The psalmist knew that perfect peace could come only by complete trust in God. Those who did this received God's favor and were assured that he would guide and keep them.

God's Help for His Anointed (20:1-9)

The psalmist composed Psalm 20 as a prayer for the king as the ruler went out to battle against formidable enemies. Many scholars see the Psalm as composed of alternate parts that should be sung by the people and king responsively. Then all would sing the chorus.

Many students, however, see a much simpler outline. They contend that in verses 1-5, the request was that God respond to the king when he prayed. In verses 6-9, the king was assured that God would hear him.

The title "A Psalm of David" may mean "concerning David," and many contend that this comes nearer to being an accurate appraisal of its meaning. Some interpreters feel that Psalm 20 was composed against the background of David's war with the Ammonites (2 Sam. 10:1-18). The reference to chariots and horses in verse 7 would refer to the Syrians who were allied with the Ammonites and helped in the battle.

Most scholars have connected Psalms 20 and 21 as companion Psalms because they are related closely in structure and content. In Psalm 20, the psalmist interceded for the king; in Psalm 21, he gave thanks for victory. In both Psalms, the king— the representative of the Lord and the people—was the prominent figure; the victory that the Lord gave to him was the leading thought.

In Psalm 20, the psalmist's main thrust was that the people loved their king and wanted him to be victorious as he fought for their common good. They recognized that the earthly sanctuary was the Lord's throne and that help had to come from God in any crisis which the nation faced. The enthusiastic bond of purpose between the people and the king, combined with their absolute reliance on the Lord, rang through the song.

In Praise of the King (45:1-17)

The psalmist composed Psalm 45 to celebrate a king's marriage to another king's daughter. He showed fine restraint as he mingled counsel and compliment with delicate tact. He avoided overdoing his praise, but he also refrained from being too austere. Most likely, the king in the psalm was Solomon; and the foreign princess probably was from Egypt (1 Kings 3:1).

This alliance cemented relationships between Israel and an important neighbor who either could be a strong ally or a dangerous enemy.

When the psalmist wrote, the kingdom was at the zenith of its glory. The people still remembered the promises to David, and their hopes for an even greater country had not been dimmed yet by failure and disappointment. In the psalm, the kingship and the kingdom were idealized, and the words were written with lofty hope.

The psalmist opened with a statement of his purpose. He bubbled over with good words as his noble subject inspired him with an impulse that he could not restrain. He addressed this preface directly to the royal bridegroom.

The first major part of Psalm 45 (vv. 2-9) recounted the glorious ways in which God had blessed the king. The ruler possessed personal beauty and gracious speech. Because he championed the cause of righteousness and justice, he always triumphed when he opposed his enemies.

The psalmist described the king's throne so graphically and affirmed the ruler's reign as so pleasing to God that the writer of Hebrews applied the description to Jesus (Heb. 1:8-10). The psalmist climaxed his description of the king by portraying the ruler on his wedding day, clothed in garments that were saturated with costly perfume which had been brought from distant lands. Music enhanced the occasion as the king entered the palace which was ornamented with costly panels.

Next, the psalmist addressed the bride (vv. 10-15). He counseled her to give reverent affection to her new lord and assured her that she would receive rich gifts. He described her magnificent appearance as she was presented to her new husband. Arrayed in her royal bridal apparel, she was conducted with stately ceremony to her new home.

Verses 16-17 were directed to the king. Although the ruler could not boast of a long ancestry, the psalmist predicted for him a numerous and distinguished posterity. The dynasty would not end with the king but would be assured of a distinguished future through the ruler's male offspring.

A Song of Messiah (110:1-7)

Appointment of Messiah (v. 1)

Psalm 110 was composed for a king's coronation. No doubt,

quoted in Mt 22:44, Acts 2:34
Heb 1:13, 5:6

across the centuries the people used it each time a new ruler was enthroned. The poem's words corresponded to the splendor of the royal celebration. The psalm opened with a message to the earthly king from the heavenly King. The psalmist dealt with the king's authority and described him as "my lord," a customary title of respect in addressing a superior but not in writing or speaking about him.

When the psalmist wrote of the king's sitting at God's right hand, he meant more than merely giving to the king a place of honor. He pointed out that the king was to share the Lord's throne, to be next to him in dignity, and to be supported by all of the forces of God's authority and power. The psalmist made this solemn declaration on God's authority, for he had received his message from the Lord. Furthermore, he promised that the king would conquer all of the foes that threatened his security. He used a figure of speech from Israel's earlier days when a conqueror put his foot on an enemy's neck as a symbol of his power (Josh. 10:24).

Who was the king? One cannot deal with Psalm 110 without recognizing how New Testament writers referred to it. In the days of Jesus, the people contended that David was the author and that the earthly king to whom David referred was the Messiah. Jesus accepted this view and used the Psalm to make clear that he was the Messiah; thus, he stamped his authority on the psalmist's words. Peter applied this verse to Christ's exaltation (Acts 2:34), and the author of Hebrews quoted it to illustrate Jesus' superiority to angels (1:13).

Alexander Maclaren showed keen insight when he wrote that Psalm 110 stands alone as not having primary reference to an earthly king. He contended: "It is not, like other Messianic Psalms, typical, but directly prophetic of Messiah, and of Him only."[1] He wrote that we must not deny the possibility of such direct prophecy. According to him, the picture that is drawn in Psalm 110 far transcends any possible original meaning among the earthly kings. He insisted that full justice is not done to its majestic picture unless one recognizes that it sets forth the personal Messiah.

Of course, the psalmist wrote in the terms of his day and against the background of earthly experiences that included a warrior-monarch approach.

Endowment of Power (v. 2)

The psalmist expanded his message and gave dignity and

strength to the king by expressing the thought of verse 1 in another bold word picture. He made clear that God would ensure that authority and divinely ordained strength came to aid the king on the battlefield. This assured the ruler that he would be backed up by all of God's effective power. He would be supported by an operative force that was capable of doing anything which was necessary to bring about the Lord's purpose.

The phrase "sends forth from Zion" (v. 2) guaranteed the new king that God's presence and resources were available to help the ruler. The new monarch should not fear because God, who dwelt in Zion, had decreed a victorious reign for him. No enemy could prevail because the rod ("scepter") of God's power, the symbol of regal authority, would fight for him. Often, Old Testament writers used the word "Zion" for the entire city of Jerusalem and, even more important, for the place where God dwelt and from which he launched his campaigns.

Help from Other Sources (v. 3)

The psalmist pointed out that the king's promised victory would not be won without human agency. As in the days of Deborah (Judg. 5:2,9), the people would be animated by a sense of loyalty to the king and would rally eagerly to his standard. The word "freely" indicated the willingness with which they would present themselves for the king's service. The Israelites regarded obeying the king's call to fight a holy war as a sacred religious duty. The psalmist already had stated clearly that the Lord's will governed the king; this gave the people added enthusiasm to help the ruler in his campaigns.

Translators vary in rendering the latter part of verse 3. The literal Hebrew reads: In the honors of holiness, from the womb, from the morning, you have the dew of your youth. Scholars have recognized this as poetical language and have interpreted as they translated, which accounts for the different renderings of the passage in the various versions. No doubt, in his description the psalmist had in mind the priests' vestments. This indicated that the warriors who volunteered their services to the Lord's anointed were performing a priestly as well as a military function. The word picture continued by comparing the freshness of the dew with the young men in holy, warlike array who placed themselves in the king's army. By this beautiful symbolic picture, the psalmist meant that God was on the king's

32

side and would send whatever aid was necessary to assure him of victory.

Priesthood of the King (v. 4)

In an even more solemn manner than in verse 1, the psalmist presented a second picture of the Lord's anointed in verse 4. God vowed so strongly to bring his work to pass concerning the Messiah that the Lord had "sworn" and would not "change his mind." When an Old Testament writer pictured God as speaking so forcefully, he did it to emphasize the certainty of the word and to stress the extreme importance of what was spoken. On several occasions, writers pictured God as changing his mind but never as changing his eternal purpose. Sometimes, the people's failure caused a temporary interruption in God's work, or at least an adjustment in his method of doing it. But God always worked toward his redemptive goal for the world. However, God would not change his mind in any way concerning his Messiah.

Verse 4 introduced a second function for the ruler: In his person and office, he would combine the work of a king and a priest. Nothing could alter this plan or cause God to amend it. The statement stressed the priestly office's eternal duration but set it apart carefully from the Levitical priests who came from Aaron's family. The king of whom the psalmist wrote would unite civil and religious life. Since he would rule "a kingdom of priests and a holy nation" (Ex. 19:6), the king would have a priestly character. Because he represented God and people, he had an office of mediation.

Melchizedek, the king of Salem, came on the scene without family. The writer of Hebrews used him to illustrate Christ's divine appointment to his office as well as the eternal duration and unique character of his function (Heb. 6:20). When the word "forever" was applied to a human ruler, it only could be fulfilled through his descendants. However, when the term applied to the Messiah, it indicated one who, like Melchizedek, had "neither beginning of days nor end of life" (Heb. 7:3). This ancient priest was king of righteousness and peace because his name literally meant king of righteousness, and he was king of Salem; the word **Salem** came from the Hebrew word *Shalom,* which meant *peace.*

Today, the world's only hope for peace is a Person, not a program. If the nations of the world ever find permanent peace,

they must find it in the Prince of Peace. I have tried to express
this thought in a poem:

> Oh, war-torn world, gone mad with strife,
> Consumed by lust and greed,
> Christ Jesus is your hope for life,
> His is the love you need.

> Men's pacts and plans will not bring peace,
> He is the only Way,
> For peace must reign in hearts of men.
> God grant it some fair day!

King in the Battlefield (vv. 5-7)

In verse 5, the scene changed to picture the king going out to
fight against his enemies. The psalmist continued to address
the king but made clear that the Lord was the ruler's champion
in the battle. The Lord was at the king's "right hand" (v. 5); this
was a figure of speech which indicated that God was helping
the king.

The word translated "will shatter" (v. 5) indicated completed
action. The writer was so sure that the event would come to
pass he wrote of it as though it already were completed. The
phrase "day of his wrath" (v. 5) referred to the time of judgment
when God would vindicate his people and his own moral laws.
In their messages, Israel's prophets and psalmists stressed
strongly the Day of the Lord. They saw it as a time when God
would show his righteousness and power.

In verse 6, the words "will execute judgment," "filling," and
"shatter" pictured action that already was completed. The
psalmist graphically saw these things happening and described
them vividly as though they already had occurred.

In verse 7, the figure of speech changed. The king rather than
the Lord was the subject of the verbs. Verses 5-6 described how
the conqueror killed the enemies; but verse 7 depicted the conqueror chasing his enemies vigorously and with success.
Though he was weary from the toil of battle and from hotly pur-
suing the enemy, the king did not quit. He halted only for a
moment to refresh himself. Then, he pressed forward to complete his victory; he did not stop until he triumphed over every
foe. The phrase **lift up his head** meant *to be successful*. The
head fell when one was faint, exhausted, disappointed,

ashamed, or defeated. When success crowned one's efforts, his head was lifted.

Psalm 110 was written against the background or conditions of its day, but its concepts were fulfilled in New Testament Christianity. In the New Testament and later, the Old Testament military terms gave way to a great missionary emphasis in spreading Christianity. In Christ, heathen nations bent before the God of love. In Jesus, the nationalistic kingdom of Israel became the spiritual kingdom of the Messiah. In the final sense, only the gospel of Christ can shatter the spear and sword and conquer the kingdoms of sin.

Lessons for Life from Psalms 2; 20; 45; 110

To rebel against God's purposes brings misery and ruin.— Our failure to accept God's will does not destroy his sovereignty. Ungodly people come on the scene and strut across the stage for a brief moment; but on history's garbage heap, they join others who, like them, have tried in vain to thwart God's plans. The wise person fits into God's plan and tries to live according to it. True happiness comes only in this way.

God is with those who are related to him.—One of the greatest resources we can possess as we enter the arena of conflict in life is a strong confidence in our ability to cope with whatever situation arises. The best way to have such confidence is to know that we are allied with God and that our lives are in harmony with his purposes. Once, during the Civil War, a group of representatives said to Abraham Lincoln: "We trust, sir, that God is on our side." He replied: "It is more important to know that we are on God's side."[2] We need human resources, but we also need to know that a little with God on our side is worth more than much without God.

God honors a good marriage.—God chose the husband and wife relationship as a symbol of the relationship between Christ and the church. Marriages do not fail. People fail by forgetting that marriage is more than *finding* the right person; it also is *being* the right person. In order to be the right person, one must be related to Christ.

When a man and a woman marry, their marriage relationship becomes the most important human relationship that they have. Their family members still are important, and the marriage partners love and care for the families from which they come. However, the husband and the wife see one another as coming first in each other's affections and priorities.

When God chooses a leader, he supports that leader.—The Lord never forsakes one whom he has called to a place of service. Sometimes the outlook may be dark, but God stands within the shadows and keeps watch over his own. If we have felt the Lord's leadership to accept a position of responsibility in his work, we can be confident that he will give us the strength to accomplish the task. What John Wesley is reported to have said on his deathbed is true, not only at the end of life but at every stage: "'The best of all, God is with us!'"[3]

1. Alexander McClaren, *The Expositors' Bible, The Psalms* (New York: Hodder & Stoughton, George H. Doran Co., n.d.), III:184.

2. Lewis C. Henry, ed., *Five Thousand Quotations for All Occasions* (Garden City, New York: Doubleday & Company, Inc., 1945), p. 107.

3. Walter B. Knight, *Knight's Master Book of New Illustrations* (Grand Rapids: Wm. B. Eerdmans Pub. Co., 1956), p. 158.

He will provide the resources AND the ability.

Personal Learning Activities

1. In Psalm 2, the psalmist expressed concern that the king's foes might overcome him. True_____ False_____
2. New Testament writers saw _____ in Psalm 2. (Select the proper response from the list.)
   (1) The church   (3) The Messiah
   (2) Little of value   (4) Beautiful poetry
3. Psalm 20 was a prayer for the king to be _____. (Choose the correct answer from the list.)
   (1) Righteous   (3) Victorious
   (2) Fair   (4) Wise
4. Psalm 45 celebrated the king's _____. (Select the correct response from the list.)
   (1) Enthronement   (3) Health
   (2) Death   (4) Marriage
5. New Testament writers applied Psalm 110 to (choose the proper answer from the list):
   _____(1) The church   _____(3) Christ
   _____(2) The gospel   _____(4) David

Answers: 1. False; 2. (3); 3. (3); 4. (4); 5. (3).

3 Songs of Praise to the Creator

Those who immerse themselves in the Psalms quickly find that praise predominates these Hebrew hymns. The songs deal with God's various attributes, his mighty deeds, and his loving concern for people. Although one section of the Psalter contains the psalms of praise, one cannot limit the inevitable impulses of a glad heart to these particular hymns. Praise to God runs through the entire book, and few psalms fail to express the psalmist's loving spirit as even lonely sadness often merges into congregational gladness. A Psalm which expresses pain may begin with throbbing hurt, but the song will end with words of rejoicing for God.

However, to the Hebrew psalmist praise was more than a passing fancy. Through the centuries, the psalms have been many things to many people. However, the songs' varied subject matter and diverse moods have one common element: Each has been crafted with love by a master of design. The psalmists' enthusiasm for God compelled them to stand before their Creator with amazement and to write so that all could understand something of his being and his acts.

In ethical content and moral impulses, the way in which the Hebrews viewed creation, even in their poetry, far surpassed the crude and fanciful narratives which came from surrounding cultures. To the psalmist, God was more than an explanation of origins. He was the ever-living One who entered history's arena through his creation. He not only brought the natural order into being, but he continued to sustain it.

Psalm 8 was written to praise God for creating the heavens, but even more to praise him for creating human personality—his highest work. Psalm 19 celebrated God's universe and praised even more highly the Law that God had given. The psalmist closed with a prayer that his words and thoughts might be acceptable to God. Psalm 29 extolled God's strength that was expressed primarily in his voice which was awesome. The psalm celebrated the God whose power ruled nature and blessed people. The psalm ended with a prayer that God would give strength to his people and bless them with peace. Psalm 65 praised God because he forgave people and sustained them. The Lord provided what they needed and blessed their daily work by providing the water that was necessary to grow grain.

If we lost every other word in the Old Testament concerning creation, the concentrated essence of the truth about God in this area of his work could be found in the Psalms. These poems serve a unique function. They bring lofty and pioneering insights about God into the common life. Thus, people can understand more deeply and praise more joyfully the God who made the earth and everything in it.

The Wonder of Persons (Psalm 8:1-9)

God's Greatness (vv. 1-2)

The psalmist wrote on behalf of the covenant people, not merely for himself or even for all mankind. The first "Lord" in verse 1 translated the name by which God revealed himself to people. The name came from a word that meant *to be* and indicated the One who always has been and always will be. The second "Lord" was from a word that meant *to rule or command*. These terms were used to show that the One whom the people knew in covenant relationship was the same One who was qualified to be ruler in every area of life. This was a fine, fitting way to express the Lord's love for his people and his sovereignty over them.

In Hebrew thinking, one's name always stood for a person's character. The term **majestic** came from a word which meant *to be wide or great*. From this meaning came the idea of magnifying or making honorable. The thought of splendor or majesty is a further but legitimate meaning. To the Israelites who were cramped by geographical boundaries and who had enemies on all sides, the idea of spaciousness or deliverance from narrow confines was important. This thought shaped their idea of salvation and their understanding of God's nature. To the psalmist, God had revealed his nature through his acts. In every land, evidences of his wisdom and grace prevailed; these evidences testified that he was more than a tribal God or God of only one race or culture.

In verse 1, the term rendered **is chanted** comes from a word that means *to render, ascribe, place, or set*. Translated literally, it expresses the psalmist's wish or prayer that God's name, so prevalent in the earth, might be exalted throughout all the heavenly world. The word "whose" which begins the clause indicates that the two phrases go together to depict adoration for and exaltation of God's person and work. The psalmist declared that God had invested even the heavenly bodies with such awesome splendor that they directed people's minds to the greatness of his creative power.

Although verse 2 shifted from the glories of the heavens to the babbling prattle of infancy and childhood, such a shift did not weaken the message. Whether the words "babes and infants" were meant literally or were used to symbolize persons' weakness, the message remained the same. God chose even the most feeble humans to be his champions. He used them to confound and silence those who refused to recognize his goodness and providence in governing the world. God erected a wall to silence his adversaries, and no one could dispute the truth that came from the most humble of his created beings.

Actually, nothing is gained by making the words "babes and infants" symbolic. A child surrenders to the impression made on him by the glorious things that he sees. Of course, a person always may broaden the application of any principle or concept that a Bible writer recorded. God endowed people with the unique faculty of speech. One Jewish writer translated Genesis 2:7: "Man became a speaking spirit." When rational beings develop the power to express their thoughts, a great step forward has been taken. Likewise, when we hear an infant's prattle, we have proof of God's creative ability.

Did the psalmist intend to include all of the Lord's foes or only those within his nation? Most likely, he had in mind those within Israel who opposed God, but the principle certainly can be extended to include all who oppose God's purposes or question his providence. The word rendered **foes** comes from a term that means *to tie up, bind, or make narrow.* From this comes the idea of *being an adversary.* The term **enemy** comes from a word which means *to be hostile to.* The word rendered **avenger** comes from a root that means *to take vengeance* and has the idea of vindictiveness. All three words indicate that the psalmist saw the opponents as active forces that were working against the Lord. The total effect of the three words suggests that they were meant to stress to all who opposed God that the opponents' work was doomed to failure. Those who were hostile or vindictive toward God were headed for ruin.

The word rendered **still** came from the same term from which the word *sabbath* came. The phrase meant that God would end the plottings of all who were against the Lord; he would cause them to refrain from their work. Through verse 2, the idea which was conveyed was that judicial function belongs to God alone, and no one can take his prerogative.

Man's Physical Insignificance (vv. 3-4)

In 8:3-4, the psalmist expanded the theme that he dealt with in verses 1-2. The splendors of darkness spoke to him concerning the God whose hand had made them. Since no mention was made of the sun, most scholars have felt that Psalm 8 was a product of thoughts that came to the psalmist at night while he was gazing at the boundless canopy of the heavens. As he saw the vastness and variety of the universe, he realized that only a skillful craftsman could have brought into being such a mysterious yet eloquent and beautiful masterpiece.

In verse 3, the word rendered **look at** literally meant *to see* and had the even stronger meaning *to perceive* or *to understand.* The psalmist did more than merely gaze at the stars and the moon. He looked with discrimination; he studied them and thought seriously about their meaning. Such an attitude led him to call them the work of God's fingers, for he knew that such a skillful piece of work could not have come from mere human power or effort. The term **established** came from a word that meant *to set up, fix, or constitute.* The term indicated direction or aim and implied purpose. This suggested that God had put each heavenly body in its appropriate sphere where it silently testified to his glory.

In verse 4, the psalmist turned from his discovery of order in the heavens, which steadied his mind, to look at the earth and its people. His twofold question about "man" and "the son of

man" was more rhetorical than interrogative. It was designed to stimulate thought; he really did not expect an answer. He was amazed that God would pay any attention to someone so weak, frail, and short-lived. In verse 4, two different Hebrew words were used for **man.** The first came from a term which meant *to be incurable, weak, sick, or mortal* and suggested the grief and sorrow of pain that endured for a day. From this came an emphasis on brevity or weakness. Included in this idea was mankind or the common person. The second word for **man** came from the term **adham** which originally meant *to be red or ruddy.* Of course, from this came the proper name *Adam;* but more specifically, the word meant a human of either sex. Later, Jesus adopted the title Son of man; but to see any messianic connection in the Psalm's words at this point is difficult. As the psalmist used it, a "son of man" meant a human offspring. Likely, no distinction was intended in the use of the two words. The first referred to the finite person; the second meant any descendant of the race.

The words in verse 4 also suggest shades of difference. The term translated **art mindful** literally means *to remember or recall,* thus, *to call to mind.* The term rendered **dost care for** comes from a word which means *to visit or attend to,* and from this *to pay attention to or observe.* This suggests the meaning *to visit.* The statement in Psalm 8 meant that God constantly held people in mind in order to look after or take care of them, which is one of the derived ideas of the word.

In verse 4, the words rendered "art mindful" and "dost care for" suggest continuous action. Thus, God does more than provide for the person's need once. He constantly watches over and keeps in mind his creation and supplies every need. The psalmist felt overwhelmed that the God who created the heavens and all the marvelous things there would give such minute attention to frail and ruddy people whose life spans were so short.

Man's Spiritual Preeminence (vv. 5-8)

In contrast to the philosophers' view, the psalmist recognized the unique truth that human dignity did not have value in itself but because it was God's gift. In verses 5-6, God was the subject. By his hand, a person was exalted in the world. This thought was pursued in great detail in order to present fully this profound truth. The psalmist recognized that one's status and limitations came from God's decree. People gained dominion over nature because God willed that all things be subject to humans—his highest creation.

Scholars differ in treating the phrase "little less than God"; many translators render the last word as "angels." The Hebrew word is *Elohim* which was used in the Semitic world for God. This word is a contrast to *Yahweh,* the name that was used for the covenant God of Israel. The author of Hebrews quoted this passage from the Greek translation of the Old Testament and used the word "angels" (Heb. 2:7). Probably, the different renderings have been made because in some instances, the Hebrew word *Elohim* has been applied generally to supernatural beings. Also, in some instances angels are called "sons of God." One should not allow the technical difficulty in translations to hide the clear message of Psalm 8. Human personality is awesome and marvelous, but the certain limitation is that people are less than God and must not forget it. However, the emphasis in verse 5 is not a warning that a person is less than God but is a tribute that one is only a little lower than God.

The phrase "thou hast made him little less than" literally reads: Thou hast caused him to lack but a little. The word translated **lack** means *to want* or *to be without anything,* but the form in which it is used gives the thrust of causing one to want or lack. The term rendered **little less than** comes from a word that means *to be or become little or few.* Combining these terms gives the thrust or meaning: "Thou hast caused him to want but little of God."[1] The psalmist viewed a person as possessing great status, even though he emphasized human frailty in verse 4.

The psalmist stressed the words **glory** and **honor.** The first comes from a Hebrew term which means *to be heavy or weighty.* From this comes the idea of having glory or honor. Actually, this Hebrew word can be translated by either "glory" or "honor." The word rendered **honor** comes from a term that means *to adorn.* Some scholars think that these terms are used interchangeably but that perhaps the latter has more of the idea of splendor or ornament. The words **dost crown** have the idea of continuity. God continues to decorate or encircle persons with dignity and status. The basic idea is *to encompass or surround.* The cumulative effect of the words "glory and honor" is to distinguish persons by giving them a status far above everything else in God's creation.

William L. Stidger wrote:

> Then to complete creation's plan
> In His own image, God made man,
> And signed His name with strokes most sure—
> Man is God's greatest signature![2]

In verse 6, the phrase "hast given him dominion" conveys the idea of continuous action. The words "hast put all things" denote completed action. This indicates that the former is in process while the latter is finished. Most likely, the statements meant that final victory has been guaranteed; thus, it is a finished matter. But God's highest creation is in the process of conquering the environment. The psalmist did not mean that God made people entirely for the purpose of subduing nature; nevertheless, God has given them power over it.

The language of verse 6b was taken from the battlefield; the picture was that of a conqueror treading down his enemies in battle and putting his feet on the captives' necks. The psalmist saw persons as exalted in authority over all other living things.

Verses 7-8 reviewed the things that were subjected to people. Even in a weak and rude state, humans have become the most dominant creatures on earth. They have investigated and utilized nature's forces which has extended their sovereignty. In attractive detail, three types of animals were pictured: those that lived in the field, those that flew in the air, and those that swam in the sea. In a sense, the phrases worked up to a climax. Each of life's three areas that people were in the process of conquering were presented as being more amazing than the previous area.

Repetition of the Opening Refrain (v. 9)
The psalmist looked back over what he had written and could think of no better way to close than with the same exclamation of reverent wonder with which he began. He repeated his words, but they had fuller significance after he meditated on how the truth that they set forth was shown so clearly. His reflecting on God and creation enabled him to see all things in their true light. As the psalmist established a correct relationship with the world and with himself, he found that this led him back to God. The amplified truth dawned on him in terms that caused him to see the creation with eyes of such deep faith that he expressed a new doxology. With adoring wonder, he again proclaimed that God's majesty shines throughout the earth so clearly that every eye can see his beauty and excellence.

The God of the Universe and of the Law (19:1-14)

God Revealed in His Works (vv.1-6)
From the outset, Psalm 19 pictured nature as a perpetual anthem. The words stressed the elements' constant witness to the Creator's unique skill. The Psalm's language clearly expressed the ever-recurring praise that the work of God's hand inspired. The word **heavens** came from an Arabic term that meant *to be high* and referred to the material elements above—the region of the sun, moon, and stars as they appeared to the eye. The word **firmament** came from a term that meant *to beat or smite the earth with the feet.* From this came the meaning *to beat out* or *to spread out or expand by beating.* The Hebrew word could mean *a strip of beaten metal.* Thus, the word "firmament" applied to the heavens as they appeared to be spread out or expanded above the earth—a mirrorlike surface.

The word translated **are telling** means *to recount or relate.*

The term **proclaim** means *to rehearse, declare, or proclaim with commendation*, which developed the idea *to praise*. Thus, the heavens recounted God's glory, and the firmament praised his artistry.

Verses 1-6 contained the general word for God, *El*, short for *Elohim*; verses 7-14 employed the term *Yahweh*, the word for Israel's covenant God. For this reason, some scholars have believed that the word "glory" possessed no moral element but simply referred to God's eternal power which indicated his existence and limitlessness.

The psalmist mentioned day and night separately because he believed that each had a special message entrusted to it and continued to proclaim that message. To him, the day told of splendor, power, and beneficence; the night spoke of vastness, order, mystery, and beauty. Like a choir's different parts, the two alternately chanted praise to God. To those who could read nature's wonders, each day became a new leaf in the record of God's continuing creation that flows like a living fountain without ceasing.

The word translated **pours forth** meant *to utter or declare*. The term rendered **declares** meant *to show*. The words conveyed the idea that each day poured out to the next the truth of God's wondrous might in the sun's rising and setting. Each night informed the next of an almighty Creator who was evidenced by the moon and stars that shone brightly in the night.

The words "pours forth" and "declares" expressed not so much the revelation's progressive character as the never-failing fact of it. The psalmist did not mean that what the day proclaimed died away and was taken up by the night. Rather, each dawning day continued the speech and each approaching night took up the story without interruption.

When the literal Hebrew reading of verse 3 is adopted, the verse means that God's work is a silent witness to his creative power.

The first part of verse 4 continued the emphasis on the universal message of God's creation. The creation's message suffered no restriction because of humanity's limited language, so both Jews and Gentiles received and understood it. Educated and uneducated people alike could comprehend it. Nature's wordless speech clearly conveyed its message. Nature spoke to the heart; therefore, its message was understood over all the earth. The psalmist's word for God emphasized the unbounded extent of the Creator's sway.

The word translated **voice** literally meant *a measuring line.* The term had the idea of *a cord, line,* or *measuring line that was used to determine a property's limit.* Verse 4 pictured it as extending to the whole world as all of the earth's inhabitants received the message. God's measuring line had taken in all the earth.

Verses 4b-6 focused attention on the sun. The sun was dealt with in a special way because people understood that the world's vitality depended on warmth, which was necessary for survival. The sun was the most prominent object among the heavenly bodies and graphically illustrated God's glory. The word "them" meant the heavens—the sun's dwelling place and one of God's most majestic works.

As the psalmist saw the fiery ball peeping over the eastern horizon, his mind turned to the bridegroom coming out of his bedchamber. This figure of speech conveyed the bright and cheerful effect of the rising sun. Joy and cheerfulness were characteristic of a man who had spent the night with his bride. The bridegroom's bouyant joy and youthful vigor, along with his feeling of strength and eagerness to prove his virility, pictured the freshness of the rising sun.

Verse 6 continued the description of the sun by showing the length of its journey. It swept the whole space of the firmament. The word "rising" came from the same term as the one translated "comes forth" in verse 5. Though the basic meaning was *to go out,* the idea of springing forth was in the word. No doubt, the psalmist chose this word in both verses to reflect his enthusiasm as he mentally pictured the sun moving out on its journey.

The word translated **circuit** means *revolution, a coming about* or *return* as the return of the seasons or the year. This exact Hebrew word is used twice where it is translated "the year's end" (Ex. 34:22) and "the end of the year" (2 Chron. 24:23). Each day, the sun makes its long journey across the heavens.

As the psalmist felt the warmth and life-giving power of the sun's rays, he concluded his description by reminding his readers of a glorious truth. God's greatest benefit, in all its brilliance, was not denied to anyone. This great splendor was described as it appeared to an onlooker who lived in his day. Whether the sun went around the earth or the earth went around the sun did not matter to the psalmist. If he had known all about modern astronomy, his basic message would not have changed. He merely would have written with deeper feeling and more reverent awe.

God Revealed in His Word (vv. 7-12)

The psalmist turned to praise a better revelation of God than the eloquent one that nature gave. In beautiful symmetry, he presented six statements (vv. 7-9) that were constructed uniformly. Each contained a name for God's special revelation, an attribute of it, and one of its effects. The synonyms (different words with the same meaning) which the psalmist used showed that he often brooded on God's teachings. Combined, the synonyms presented a meaningful group of qualities that a devout person would see in God's Word. To wicked people, the qualities of the Lord's law would be only restraints.

The Psalm's rhythm and structure were changed in verses 7-12; a meter was introduced which was like that of an elegy (a pensive and reflective poem). In today's English translations, one can see how each line is divided into a longer part and a shorter part. One can feel the psalmist's heart beat with increased joy as he wrote about God's Word. The literary scheme of the verses suggests that he drew deeper breaths as he wrote. His spirit rose and fell like the sea's waves because the special revelation of God's Word inspired him more than nature's general voice.

God's revelation (vv. 7-9).—In verse 7, the psalmist began his description of God's truth with the familiar term **torah** which was rendered *law*. This word came from a term that meant *to teach*. In its broader application, **torah** included all of God's instructions regarding conduct; therefore, it was applied to all of the knowledge that God has communicated to people rather than exclusively to his commands.

The term **perfect** comes from a word that means *to complete or finish*. Thus, the word teaches that God's revelation lacks nothing in order to show people what they should be in life's daily duties. God's teaching is a flawless guide which will not mislead or fail a person.

The word **reviving** (v. 7) came from a term that meant *to turn or return*; the prophets used this word often as they called people back to God. The psalmist saw that when God's instruction was accepted, it brought a person from the error of his/her ways to pursue a holy life. It caused one to return to wholeness or to be refreshed.

The term **soul** (v. 7) is the Hebrew word *nephesh* that refers to one as a total personality. This picture was placed first in the list because it was considered to be the primary design of God's speaking to those whom he created in his image. God's flawless teaching was designed to restore one's life.

In the second part of verse 7, the word **testimony** meant *that which was borne witness to* or *that which one declared to be true.* Often the word was used of the two tables of the Law in the ark called the ark of the testimony. The psalmist contended that what God said was not unsettled, variable, or vascillating; it was well established and unshakable, and it could be relied on for firmness. The term "simple" referred to one whose mind was open to the coming of good or evil. This person did not have a mind that was closed against instruction, but the individual also had no fixed principles to aid in resisting temptation. Such a one needed instruction because he/she could be impressed by wrong. Unless such a person was made wise by God's Word, that individual might take a foolish path.

In verse 8, the word "precepts" referred to the mandates or special injunctions that stated clearly one's obligation; they were given to guide people's conduct. If these rules were followed properly, they would bring happiness that flowed from moral satisfaction and a clear conscience.

In the latter part of verse 8, the word **commandments** came

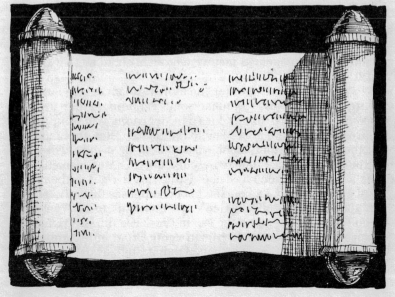

from a term that meant *to set up, constitute, or order.* The psalmist did not mean that the thing was right in itself as much as he meant that it was ordered by God; it was what God required. It was God's imperative—a statutory deliverance—so it became the general term for a law in religious life that summed up a person's whole duty. The term **pure** meant *free from all stain, imperfection, or corrupt tendency.* As the sun gave light to the world, God's commandments gave light to people in their moral search. The term "eyes" was used because eyes saw the path which a person traveled. No doubt, the thought was that the mind or soul was enlightened by God's truth.

In the list of synonyms for Law, "fear" (v. 9) was not the external act demanded, effected, and maintained by God's revelation. God's Commandments were designed to implant reverence in people's hearts—to make them pious. This feeling was intended to give direction to people's actions since their deeds should correspond to their feelings about God.

The word **clean** (v. 9) meant *clear or pure in a physical sense* as distinguished from filthy or soiled. Ceremonially, the word was opposed to that which was profane or common; morally, it was the opposite of anything that corrupted or defiled one's life. Every idea connected with the term related to a holy tendency that was adapted to cleanse a person's life and make one capable of fellowship with God. Such a state never would decay or pass away. The immoralities of heathenism could not produce a life that endured. Only one who held proper respect for God and lived out the implications of such an attitude could withstand the consequences that were brought about by the passing of time.

In the latter part of verse 9, the term **ordinances** comes from a word which means *to judge.* Some versions render it *judgments.* This word stands for right decisions which in themselves make up a body of law for guidance. They are the result of the divine verdict about what is best for people. The term "true" suggests that they represent reality. These judgments are not arbitrary but are consistent with what is right in the moral and ethical realm. Of course, this presupposes that an absolute standard exists and that God's law conforms to it. What God said is true; it has stood the test of time. The phrase "righteous altogether" means that a person cannot find an exception in God's administration of justice. All that God has determined is correct and best for people; therefore, it is worthy of universal confidence.

The value of God's revelation (vv. 10-12).—The psalmist esteemed God's law as the ultimate value and the supreme good. He ranked it higher than all earthly treasures and pleasures. In verses 7-9, he wrote of its worth in the abstract; in verses 10-11, he gave his feelings regarding it. He esteemed it more than the most prized objects among people. The word translated "gold" was the ordinary term that indicated that which was bright or fair. The words **fine gold** meant *gold that had gone through a purifying process.* The psalmist used this comparison to show that God's revealed truth was/is a treasure above all which people could accumulate. He recognized that spiritual riches were superior to material wealth as a means of obtaining joy and fulfillment in life.

Verse 10*b* compared the Law with one of the most delicate satisfactions that the body could enjoy. Too much honey might sate one and produce a sickening effect; but the more one received God's word and applied it to life, the stronger one's character became. The word translated "honey" was the ordinary one in Hebrew, but the phrase "drippings of the honeycomb" referred to the honey that overflowed, which was the purest. When one pressed the combs, a mixture of beebread almost inevitably came. However, the part which flowed naturally from the comb was unadulterated. Thus, in these two figures of speech the Law was portrayed as a treasure to be coveted as the sweetest of enjoyments.

The psalmist understood the value of counsel and admonition. In verse 11, the word **warned** meant *to instruct and admonish.* The term's essential idea was to throw light on the subject or to show it clearly in order to make one's duty plain and the consequences clear. Pious people knew the risk of ignoring God's teachings and the value of heeding the signposts that the Lord erected along the road.

The psalmist knew that the Law acted as a prison and spoiled the wicked persons' coarse gratifications. Those who disobeyed God felt that life was barred wearisomely from the joys and delights that sin seemed to promise. Furthermore, he knew that those who stayed behind the fences which the Law set up warded off those evils and, within that security, enjoyed pure pleasures that only God could give.

People do not lose anything when they shun evil methods of gaining riches. Neither do they forfeit the best in life when they adopt purity as their moral standard; they gain what really counts in life.

The reward for keeping God's commands is both present and future. Joy comes in the day-by-day acts of doing God's will, but it is not limited to this area. Future security is made more certain by living according to the standards that God has established. The language in verse 11 implied both rewards. The phrase "thy servant" suggests that through experience, the psalmist had found his statements to be true.

In verse 12, the word **errors** came from a term that meant *to wander or go astray*. The psalmist wrote of sins that were not willful—mistakes that one made without being aware of them. He knew that though a person might be eager to serve God, no one was without fault or stumbling. God's Law was so pure, holy, and strict in its demands that no one could recall every departure that he/she made from its requirements.

The psalmist not only conceded his inability to remember every shortcoming, but he also prayed to be forgiven. The term **clear** came from a word that meant *to be pure or innocent*. In the form that the poet used in verse 12, it meant *to cleanse, pronounce innocent, acquit, or pardon*. The psalmist took sin seriously and prayed to be purified from every hidden fault. He recognized that the test of one's religious faith was the struggle against every sin—those that others knew, and those that the individual knew or was unaware of.

Joseph Parker compared hidden sins to the white ants in Africa that had enormous powers to destroy as they worked insidiously and secretly. He told how one could sit in a hut, thinking that it was as strong as the day it was built, but suddenly only a shell remained. He said that silently, the white ants had been at work eating out the heart of every beam. No one saw them, heard them as they worked, or had any warning of their presence. Suddenly, however, the pillars of the house trembled and the secret ravages became visible. Sins about which people think no one knows, and which sometimes even the individuals themselves do not realize, suddenly burst out on them in full judgment.

Protection from Presumptuous People (v. 13)

Although almost every translator renders the Hebrew word in verse 13 as "presumptuous sins," the normal translation would be: presumptuous ones—the arrogant and godless persons. If this be accepted, the psalmist prayed for protection from the presumptuous people's oppression because it could lead him to doubt or even to deny God. Most likely, however, he meant to give a contrast to the "hidden faults" of verse 12. The word from which the phrase **presumptuous sins** came meant *to act insolently, proudly, or rebelliously against one.* Actually, the term did not refer to people with open or flagrant sins as much as to sins which sprang from self-reliance or pride. The psalmist prayed that he might distrust himself properly in order that he might not depend on his own power to avoid sin. He wanted to be certain that such attitudes and acts never mastered him. He did not want to become sin's slave or to allow it to dominate him. He knew that only the righteous person had true freedom.

The word translated "shall be blameless" is the basis for the term "perfect" in verse 7; it describes the "law of the Lord." The word does not imply sinless perfection; it denotes wholeness, uprightness, sincerity, and integrity.

A Prayer for Acceptance (v. 14)
In verse 14, the psalmist closed by stating his aspiration that the Lord would accept his song and prayer. The phrase "be acceptable" occurred often in connection with sacrificial ritual, but the psalmist gave it a spiritual meaning. A few versions followed the Septuagint and read: "always acceptable." This would follow the demand that the daily sacrifice be offered continually (Ex. 29:38-42).

Psalm 19 closed with two figures of speech that referred to the Lord. The term "rock" referred to the security that the people sought in times of danger. The dark caves became places of refuge where they fled from the enemy. Such places abounded in the land. The word translated "redeemer" was a term that was used for the nearest of kin who was to buy the property of a widow in financial difficulty and thus to keep it from passing outside the family. Both of these terms had special significance for the people of the day in which the Psalm was written and were meaningful when they were applied to the covenant God of Israel.

The God of Power (29:1-11)

The psalmist was a religious genius who saw in a great thunderstorm the Lord's might and majesty. With realistic effect, he presented a verbal symphony which reproduced in words the thunder's shattering peals that echoed around the hills. Although the tempest brought terrors, the psalmist interpreted the roaring elements as God's majestic voice and remained calm. He knew that he did not need to dread the elements because God who possessed infinite goodness, truth, mercy, and love controlled them.

Psalm 29 unfolds dramatically in three scenes. The first is the prelude (vv. 1-2) which takes place in the heavenly court. The psalmist did not try to describe the Lord but called on the "heavenly beings" (v. 1) to render their praise to him. The Hebrew phrase *sons of God (Elohim)* has caused difficulty for the translators. Some prefer to render it sons of might or sons of power since the Hebrew word for God comes from a term which means strength. However, the psalmist stressed not only God's strength but also his glory and holiness.

The second section (vv. 3-9) made clear that the psalmist looked at nature from a religious viewpoint. He did not contemplate its wonder, beauty, and variety for its own sake or as an end in itself. All the world spoke to him of God's power, glory, and love. Nature supplied him with figures of speech to proclaim God's attributes and his works in history. Thus, he saw the thunder as God's voice and the storm as an expression of the majesty that the universe's eternal Sovereign had.

In describing the storm, the psalmist referred to the thunder seven times as the "voice of the Lord." He viewed it as "upon the waters" (v. 3), "powerful" (v. 4a), and "full of majesty" (v. 4b). He described how the Lord's voice broke the cedars (v. 5), flashed forth flames of fire (v. 7), and shook the wilderness (v. 8). The poet's final picture was twofold: The Lord's voice made the oaks to whirl and stripped the forests bare (v. 9). The cumulative effect of the Lord's voice caused everyone in the sanctuary to shout praise to God's glory.

In the final section (vv. 10-11), the psalmist meditated on the storm that had passed. From this incident, he knew that the Lord controlled all floods and was unequalled in power. Since this was true, the Lord could give to his people the ability to cope with any emergency that might come. The psalmist put his confidence in the One who could arm himself with such power and control the elements. He prayed for the Lord to give the people resources that were necessary to make their lives full and happy.

The God Who Provides (65:1-13)

The allusions to the people's gathering in the Temple (vv. 2,4) indicate that Psalm 65 was written for one of Israel's three great festivals. Since verse 13 pictures the corn as still in the fields, some scholars exclude Pentecost or Tabernacles and hold that the song was intended to be sung at Passover. The two psalms that follow combine with Psalm 65 to form a cluster that conveyed one dominant thought: God's grace and providence to Israel as a witness to the world. The psalmist made God the focal point as he delighted in the blessings that the Lord sent to make life joyful. Probably, he composed the poem after some national disaster, possibly a drought, a military invasion, or both.

The first section (vv. 1-4) deals almost completely with God's glory in answering prayer. The psalmist felt that grateful people should gather in God's house to offer thanks to the One who heard their petitions. Sin made people unfit to approach God, but forgiveness came to those who sought it. In this section, the people were pictured in reverential silence as they looked forward to the thanksgiving service's beginning. The entire nation enjoyed access to God and found joy as they worshiped in his house.

The second section (vv. 5-8) relates how God provides safety in national crises. Some scholars believe that the psalmist composed this hymn shortly after the nation's deliverance from the Assyrian Sennacherib's seige of Jerusalem. This was during Isaiah's time.

The second section celebrated God's wonderful deeds which brought the world into being. The emphasis on God as Creator suggested the thanksgiving theme. In the beginning, God created the world; but he also continued to sustain it.

The third section (vv. 9-13) enhanced the thought of continued creation. God sent refreshing rains on the earth which caused corn to spring up, grass to grow, and the hills to rejoice. The psalmist wrote at the joyful time when summer's beauty touched the earth and the harvest still was a glorious hope. The beauty of it filled his song with exultation. He could view the white fleeces of the flocks that dotted the meadow and could not see the ground because of the tall corn that waited for the sickle. He felt that he could hear a hymn of glad praise rising from nature, and he gave a vivid picture of a joyous landscape that was rich with promise. This graphic and vivid description of the psalmist's hearing the hidden tones of the spring symphony expressed his and his people's gratitude. He proclaimed his thanks for God's external blessings as well as for inward union with the Lord—the most precious fruit of worship.

Lessons for Life from Psalms 8; 19; 29; 65

God sees much in every person.—Although the Bible teaches that all people are sinners, this is not the full story. Every person has infinite worth in God's sight. Sin has separated people from their Maker, and no one can attain fullness without Jesus Christ as Savior and Lord. Nevertheless, every person has possibilities for development.

No person can claim that he/she knows nothing about God.—Although some know more about him than others, everyone has seen some evidences of God. Paul's conclusion was that even the heathen knew enough about God from creation that they were "without excuse" (Rom. 1:20). All of the people in the world are guilty of sin and must be saved.

God's holiness is beautiful and should lead people to worship.—God's courage, morality, unselfishness, and love stand out as some of the loveliest and most desirable qualities that people can possess. People become like that which they worship.

God delivers his people from crisis if they will trust him.—Sometimes one may feel neglected by God, but always he stands "within the shadow, keeping watch above his own."[3] God never forsakes those who belong to him. The waiting time is difficult, but vindication always comes.

[1]Albert Barnes, "The Book of Psalms." *Notes on the Old Testament* (Grand Rapids, Michigan: Baker Book House, 1981), I:71.

[2]*I Saw God Wash the World* (Chicago: The Frederick H. Jaenicken Co. Pubs., 1934), p. 12.

[3]James Russell Lowell, "The Present Crisis."

Personal Learning Activities

1. Psalm 8 celebrated the wonder of _____. (Choose the correct answer from the list.)
   (1) The Law   (3) Persons
   (2) The angels   (4) The king
2. In Psalm 19, the psalmist held that _____ and _____ revealed God. (Select the proper answers from the list.)
   (1) The universe   (3) The Temple
   (2) Human beings   (4) The Law
3. In Psalm 29, the psalmist saw in a thunderstorm God's wrath. True_____ False_____
4. Psalm 65 celebrated God's _____. (Choose the proper answer from the list.)
   (1) Holiness   (3) Power
   (2) Righteousness   (4) Provision
5. In the last section of Psalm 65, the psalmist celebrated God's sending needed rain. True_____ False_____

_____

4 Songs for a Nation

Although the psalmists often wrote about their personal problems and needs, many times they lamented their nation's woes and tribulations. From the beginning, the Israelites maintained a community consciousness; they looked on the entire people as a corporate personality. Many psalmists reflected this feeling as they prayed that God would turn the people's fortunes and bring prosperity.

As the memory of disappointed hopes grew, the desire for a new period in God's dealing with his people became intense. When the nation fell on hard times, the psalmists confessed for the people in beautiful songs. Many national laments in the Psalter almost seem to have been political in nature. In these songs, the Lord's people were depicted as a small colony in great distress; the people were sighing under the oppression of ill-disposed neighbors. Offensive speech from their enemies tended to arouse bitter verbal clashes. Through their psalmists, the Lord's people cried out for deliverance.

The four poems that were chosen for this study illustrate national difficulty. In Psalm 12, a godless society caused the psalmist to ask God for protection. All around were arrogant people who spoke lies and caused the people to fear. Psalm 14 affirmed the fact that God lives, and one who denied his existence was foolish. This song was a prayer of deliverance for Israel; nevertheless, at the end, it breathed a spirit of certainty. Psalm 80 was a prayer for Israel's Shepherd to deliver the nation; only God could bring the restoration that the severe crisis made necessary. Unspecified national difficulty formed the background for Psalm 85. Although the crisis was not identified, it was viewed as God's judgment on the nation. After a recounting of past blessings, a plea was made for God to deliver the nation once more; then, the conviction was stated strongly that the prayer for deliverance would be answered.

Prayer for Protection (12:1-8)

Those who live close to God face pain because they feel deeply about moral issues. Psalm 12 was composed by one who saw the almost universal hypocrisy that accompanied the nation's decay. Although the psalmist suffered, he was concerned more deeply about what sin was doing to the land.

When was Psalm 12 composed? Most scholars place it during David's lifetime. Some suggest that David wrote it during his young manhood while he was fleeing from Saul's armies; others point to Absalom's rebellion when many of David's trusted friends turned against him.

Some interpreters see verses 1-4 as a prayer for help because evil was prevalent everywhere. Like Elijah, the psalmist felt alone as God's servant. He singled out sins of speech as being prevalent in the land. In verse 5, God answered the plaintive cry and promised to give security to those who had been made to suffer. Prophecy and psalmody met as the psalmist addressed

God and as God answered the people through him. God gave his instructions for the people to one who delivered the Lord's word as an authoritative message. Verses 6-8 expressed confidence in God's answer. Unlike the people's deceitful words, God's words could be trusted. Human speech might contain both truths and lies; but, repeatedly, God's Word had been proved to be pure. The expression of certainty ended with a prayer that God would defend the people from the evil ones who sought to exploit the weak and oppressed. Divine intervention was necessary to curb the widespread depravity in the land. Deep faith expressed itself; at the same time, the petition continued.

Prayer for Deliverance (14:1-7)

General Depravity Asserted (v. 1)

The psalmist wasted no time in getting to his subject. He viewed the human scene; then, with great energy he pictured the root cause for the evil in the land. He traced this deep and universal source of wickedness to the people's failure to seek God—or seemingly even to believe that he existed. In verse 1, the term *Elohim*, the general word for God, was employed. In the remaining verses, the term *Yahweh*, the covenant name for Israel's God, was used. In using the general word for God, the psalmist may have referred not merely to Israel but to all nations as he looked at the moral corruption in his day.

The word **fool** comes from a term that means *to wither, fade, or fall off*, as leaves and flowers faded and fell. A further meaning is *to lose one's strength* or *to act foolishly*. The word "fool" does not refer to one who is mentally weak or academically inferior, but rather to a person whose moral judgments are deficient. To the Hebrews, the fool was one who lacked honor and decency and who preferred wicked conduct to righteous conduct.

On the other hand, wisdom always referred to character; folly never was removed far from sinful and wicked acts. Of course, an element of intellectual understanding was essential to wisdom, but the Jews did not stress this part as much as the Greeks did. A fool was not a speculative atheist but one who lived as though God did not judge people's deeds.

The words "are corrupt" and "do abominable deeds" stress

making something to be or become. The terms indicated that the people already had engaged in the deeds and had brought them to fruition. This did not mean that the actions were no longer in process; rather, the emphasis was placed on the final product that came from the people's terrible actions.

Depraved people have no desire for God because they want to lead wicked lives. Those who desire to live righteously "seek after God" (v. 2). Only corrupt people find pleasure in an argument that proposes to disprove God's existence. A practical atheist seeks to escape from the demands which God's reality makes on one's life; he or she lives as if God did not exist. Continued disobedience results in an inability to do what is good. The destiny that awaits those who sense no duty to God is to abandon all belief in God and to practice that which God abhors.

The terms that were used to describe the people's character pictured individuals who were unrestrained by belief in God as Sovereign. Therefore, such people became those who wished to have the last word about what was right and wrong. When people denied God by their daily practices, two forms of evil resulted: (1) They made their doings rotten to themselves and loathsome to those who held high ideals because of their belief in God. (2) They refrained from good deeds.

The psalmist came to a dreary estimate of those about him. He felt that the entire world was void of even one righteous person. In Hebrew, the statement in verse 3 reads: There is not a doer of good. The psalmist felt completely alone in a world that was rebelling against God.

Prevalent Sinfulness Illustrated (vv. 2-3)

The psalmist moved quickly into the exalted region where God dwells. Many psalmists made this quick shift from human life's noisy fuss to divine quiet. However, stillness never meant inactivity or unawareness. Just as human beings could do, God could stand and stare. The words "looks down" denoted completed action; the Lord already had surveyed the scene and had reached his verdict. The research was complete; therefore, God's decision was correct. The Hebrew word translated "looks down" conveyed the idea of bending forward and looking intently. The psalmist meant that God had scrutinized closely in order to secure a correct appraisal. Through intense study, he wanted to ascertain people's moral condition. He looked at the people with their pretended goodness, and he saw none who were not depraved.

The phrase "children of men" (v. 2) could be translated: sons of Adam. The phrase indicated the human race—all of the descendants of the person whom God originally created. The Old Testament writers frequently used the phrase to describe collectively all of the people who lived in the world. The word translated **act wisely** expressed continuous action. The term meant *to be upright* or *to be pious.* The word **maskil,** which came from the term employed in verse 2, was used as a title or description of several psalms (32; 42; 44); it meant a devout or didactic poem (a poem designed to teach). In verse 2, the psalmist contrasted wise action with the folly that he referred to in verse 1. God searched for godly or pious people.

The term **seek** expressed continuous action and meant *to search for, ask,* or *inquire.* A further meaning was to apply oneself or to promote the welfare of anyone. God looked for persons who applied themselves to asking or inquiring about him and his standards of living.

God had revealed himself through the voice of conscience and the works of creation, but the people had not followed the light within or read the book of nature. God's all-seeing eye searched the entire human race in order to find one who showed discernment and thus considered fellowship with God as the highest good. From his search, God came to a pessimistic conclusion which the psalmist recorded.

The word translated **gone astray** (v. 3) meant *to turn aside* or *away* and thus *to depart.* When it described one's rejecting God and his laws of righteousness, it meant *to become degenerate.* Even though God conducted a lenient search to find good people, the shocking result was that all had wandered from the path of righteousness. The word translated **alike** basically meant *altogether, wholly.* The implication of the word in verse 3 meant that sinful people encouraged one another in wickedness, and evil gained momentum as it fed on itself.

The word translated "corrupt" (v. 3) comes from a term that means *to become sharp* or *sour,* as milk that spoils. From this comes the idea of corruption in a moral sense.

In verse 3, the psalmist repeated his affirmation of universal depravity that he stated in verse 1 but added another phrase for emphasis. The Hebrew literally reads: not even one. At this point, Psalm 14 showed vigor as it gave the second step in the practical atheist's development. Deeds had turned on and poisoned the person who committed them; that individual lived as though God did not exist.

Certain Retribution Promised (vv. 4-6)

Next, the psalmist wrote against particular abuses in the land. He did so by recording words that the Lord spoke. God spoke with utter amazement in an outburst of indignation. The Hebrew text of verse 4 began with an expression that could be rendered "surely"; if so, the psalmist felt that for wicked people to feel that God would overlook their behavior was inconceivable. The expression **evildoers** literally meant *practicers of iniquity*. The word "iniquity" in verse 4 has the basic meaning of *nothingness, lightness, or easiness*. From this comes the idea of vanity, falsehood, wickedness, and thus iniquity.

The psalmist asked his rhetorical question in verse 4 to reveal the folly of those who showed no concern for God or his people. The sentence sounds like a last-minute appeal for them to realize the utter absurdity of their conduct.

Some scholars have felt that the phrase "eat up my people" (v. 4) meant that the wicked individuals used the righteous people's inconsistencies to confirm the evil persons' denial of God's existence. More likely, however, the psalmist referred to people with a total absence of religious and social responsibility who exploited the weak and oppressed. They ruined their fellow countrymen, and they cared nothing for God's commandments. The expression "eat bread" may have been more than a mere metaphor. The greedy sinners lived by fattening themselves on the spoils that they looted from their prey. The phrase "my people" may have referred to Israel's being exploited by foreigners; or, it may have meant that the righteous persons in Israel were plundered by the unrighteous people of the nation.

The phrase "do not call upon the Lord" (v. 4) makes clear that all of the iniquities which the evil people committed sprang from their rejecting God. When one rules God out, many different kinds of sins arise. The evil people's problem was that they tried to live as though they owed allegiance to no one. All other sins came from this fact and were subordinate to it.

In verse 5, the psalmist clearly stated that wherever God chose to manifest his judgment on the wicked people, dread would overwhelm them. The first phrase of the verse could be rendered: They feared a fear. This reading indicated great terror. The evil persons' practical atheism brought no calm or peace. They tried to convince themselves that since God did not exist, they had nothing to dread; but they could not do so. In spite of their efforts, proofs of God's existence abounded and caused them to tremble.

The psalmist clearly indicated that God's reality could not be removed or evaded by shutting one's eyes to it. In the future, people would become aware of God's presence too late. Panic stricken, they would realize that God had confronted them as an adversary because he only was with those who sought to live by his standards. The phrase "generation of the righteous" (v. 5) is synonymous with the words "my people" in verse 4. The phrase either referred to the nation which was described as righteous because it was called to the messianic mission or to the godly part of it.

In verse 6, the Lord spoke through the psalmist directly to the wicked concerning their base conduct. In the Hebrew text, the phrase "plans of the poor" occurs first in the sentence; this structure emphasizes how important to God the poor people were. The word rendered **plans** came from a term that meant *to consult*. The phrase indicated the reliance of the afflicted persons on God's justice and condemned those who derided the poor people's dependence as mere folly. The word **confound** meant *to make one ashamed, confused, or perplexed*. The wicked people already were confusing and exploiting their victims.

The evildoers sought to cut off every hope that the righteous people had and to leave them in despair by putting out the last glimmer of light concerning God. However, the psalmist wrote like a prophet and hurled at them the threatening truth that the Lord would confound human sin.

The basic truth in verse 6 is that those who put their trust in the Lord will be protected and never will be disappointed. The entire section (vv. 4-6) contains assurance from the Lord to his confused and bewildered people.

Complete Deliverance Petitioned (v. 7)

The destiny that awaited God's people pressed heavily on the psalmist's soul. His anxious sorrow caused him to reveal an insight into his own heart. The word translated "O" was a question—"Who?"—but it took the form of a prayer: Who will give out of Zion salvation to Israel? Verse 7 was more than a mere addition to the poem for worship purposes. The song needed a positive conclusion. To have ended with verse 6 would not have been in keeping with the spirit that the psalmist breathed into other parts of the song. Today, a reader almost can feel a brief pause after verse 6 and sense the choir raising an intense and passionate prayer for God to change the people's fortunes.

The psalmist realized that any redemption had to come directly from the Lord. He also sensed that such activity would proceed from Zion where God dwelt and from which he issued his commands and exercised his power. One does not need to suppose that the words referred to a literal captivity such as the time Israel spent in Babylon. The people often were subjected to oppression, and such an expression became the common method to designate any troublesome time. As the psalmist looked to God, his faith again prevailed. He realized that judgment was/is never God's last word. Although even God's people had to suffer because of their sins, the Lord would forgive them and bring them out of their present dilemma. Verse 7 made the Psalm a valuable testimony because it expressed one person's faith and assurance.

Some scholars have seen a messianic hope in verse 7 as the psalmist anticipated Israel's destiny of great joy. Those who understood the true nature of the nation's mission well could have seen such a truth in the words of the verse. God continued to deliver his people because he had chosen them to be his agents for worldwide mission. Redeemed people always exult in the Lord! How can they do otherwise? And they rejoice as they work in God's redemptive purpose.

The Nation's Shepherd (80:1-19)

Psalm 80 can be divided into three divisions: verses 1-3, 4-7,8-19. This is based on the identical verse in each division which begins, "Restore us, O God," and appears at each section's close.

Verses 1-3 expressed a prayer for God to show his favor to the Northern Kingdom by restoring the nation's past prosperity. The Lord was addressed as "Shepherd of Israel" (v. 1). This thought runs through the entire Psalm, though the expression does not occur again. God also was pictured as one "enthroned upon the cherubim" (v. 1), and the prayer was made that the Lord would stir up his power and let his countenance glow so that Israel might be delivered.

In verses 4-7, the psalmist expressed surprise at God's continued dissatisfaction which was evidenced by the suffering which abounded. He complained that the Lord had chastised the people; God had ridiculed them in the presence of those who lived nearby and had made them an object of derision to their foes. Verse 7 repeated the prayer for deliverance that was stated in verse 3.

Verses 8-13 compared Israel to a vine that God set up when he brought the people out of Egypt and defeated the Canaanites. At first, God watched over the young nation carefully; then, he gave the people over to ferocious beasts who exploited them.

Verses 14-17 contain an impassioned plea that God would restore his desolate creation. Verse 18 expresses Israel's promise that if God delivered the people, they would not stray again. The final prayer in verse 19—or the repetition of verses 3 and 7—concludes the Psalm.

People who want an exact literary style and balanced stanzas with repeating phrases will not find it in Psalm 80. The spiritual message is paramount, not the literary arrangement. Probably, the worshiping community recited this Psalm when the tribes came together at the central shrine. The psalmist's distress at plundered cities stood out, and his artistry was revealed by his figures of speech. He wove together allegory and its application as he presented his longing for God to restore the people. He began and closed with a petition, but his mood rose into a certainty that God would hear him. The psalmist reached the peak of his thoughts and feelings in verse 18 when he vowed that the hoped-for consummation would cause Israel to turn back to the Lord.

Revive Us Again! (85:1-13)

Acknowledgment of Past Deliverance (vv. 1-3)

The Book of Nehemiah forms an excellent background for Psalm 85. Earlier, the people had returned from Babylonian captivity, had rebuilt the Temple, and had enjoyed many blessings from God. Later, however, they turned away from the Lord; in Nehemiah's day, they suffered for it. They needed a fresh outpouring of spiritual strength which the psalmist knew could come only from God.

In verses 1-3, the words "wast favorable," "didst restore," "didst forgive," "didst pardon," "didst withdraw," and "didst turn" were placed first in the sentences to give the terms strong emphasis. The psalmist remembered former events with gratitude, and he wrote Psalm 85. Most likely, he meant for the congregation to sing it antiphonally at one of the nation's great religious festivals. He sought to focus the people's thoughts firmly on God as they expressed gratitude to the Lord for his mighty acts of past deliverance. Probably, included in the song of praise was a reference to the immediate past; however, the reference was not limited to any one event. The psalmist's mind stretched across the centuries to the many deliverances that God had worked for the people.

The term translated **wast favorable** basically means *to delight, take pleasure in, be pleased with,* or *accept kindly or graciously.* The psalmist did not mean that God was pleased with the sin that the people had committed which brought them to their plight. Rather, the meaning was that God heard their plea for pardon and decided that they had suffered long enough.

The word translated **didst restore** is the same one that the prophets used when they called the nation to repentance. The term means *to turn* or *return,* and the text literally reads: Thou didst turn (return) the captivity of Judah. Although it is not stated specifically, the words imply that the people had shown heart-felt sorrow for sin which prompted God's willingness to restore them.

In verse 2, the psalmist used two striking words for wrongdoing and two equally striking ones for God's removal of the misdeeds. The term translated "iniquity" emphasized wickedness as moral corruption or perversity. The word also had the idea of guilt and punishment for that wickedness. The word **sin** meant *to miss one's step, stumble,* or *fall.* Actually, this word was not as strong or forceful as some of the other words that were used for ungodly behavior. It did not necessarily imply a rebellious attitude; rather, it implied coming short in seeking to reach a standard.

The word **forgive** (v. 2) comes from a term that means *to lift or raise up.* From this comes the idea *to bear* or *to take away.* When it is applied to one's sin, the word means *to bear one's guilt or take away the person's sin.* The word **pardon** has the basic idea *to cover over or conceal.* As the psalmist presented sin under two figures of speech, he also presented God's merciful dealing with sin in two ways. To him, wickedness was a crushing burden that needed to be lifted and carried away; and it was a missing of the mark that needed to be covered over or

67

forgiven.

In verse 3, two vivid words were used to indicate God's removing his displeasure with the people's conduct. The verb **withdraw** meant *to take in, draw back as with the hand, and to take away.* The psalmist conveyed the idea that God dealt with his people in such a way as to make clear that he was not displeased with them. He had drawn back or taken away his wrath. The word translated "didst turn" was the same as the one in verse 1 ("restore"), except that it conveyed a bit firmer and more resolute action.

The word **wrath** (v. 3) conveys the idea of *going over in order to accomplish certain actions.* The word applies to many situations, one of the most prevalent of which is to exercise justifiable vengeance on those whose pride has incurred displeasure. The phrase "hot anger" consists of two interesting Hebrew words. The term **hot** is from a word which means *to burn, be kindled, or become angry.* The term **anger** comes from a word which means *to breathe through the nose or snort.* From this comes the idea of being or becoming angry. God turned from a burning agitation with his people.

The overall thrust in Psalm 85:1-3 was a great affirmation of faith. The psalmist wrote for the people and gratefully acknowledged the nation's past that was so rich in tokens of God's favor. This grateful recollection at the beginning of the song expressed God's interest in the nation that was called the Lord's land (v. 1). The psalmist traced to God's goodness the people's past prosperity. Although the thought was not stated, the people's present distress probably was regarded as an illustration of the troubles which came when people were unfaithful to God. Grateful memories like the psalmist's brought inspiration and promoted healthy-mindedness in religion. Today, such memories still should inspire healthy religion.

Prayer for Present Plight (vv. 4-7)

The Psalm moved to an urgent request for God to extend anew the loving-kindness that he had shown in former days. The quick shift from the backward look at God's grace to a petition for the Lord's putting away his anger seems abrupt. However, prophets and psalmists often adopted this technique. Disappointment caused leaders to present bold hopes for salvation. The psalmist confronted the tension of his day with an attitude which all genuine faith exhibits.

The word translated **restore us** (v. 4) could be rendered *return* us. If so, the psalmist first prayed for God to make the people repent and become willing to forsake their evil ways. Also, the prayer would ask God to give enabling power to the people. The psalmist did not pray first for God to take away his (the Lord's) wrath; rather, he asked God to lead the people to forsake their sins and turn to God.

The word **put away** (v. 4) means *to declare void, annul, or abolish*. The term "indignation" comes from a word that means *to be provoked or angry*. The psalmist wasted no words and spoke boldly as he pleaded for God to turn from his wrath against the people—to make void his anger.

The two questions in verse 5 probably should be considered rhetorical (questions that expected no answers) or at least ones that expected negative answers. One might translate: You are not going to be angry with us forever, are you? Surely you are not going to continue your anger toward us to all later generations! The word **prolong** means *to draw out, stretch, or hold out the hand*. The psalmist realized that unless God showed mercy to the people, they could not rebuild their national life. Even a partial restoration would not be enough. God had to cease his wrath completely, and the psalmist urged him to do so. He pleaded that God's judgment might end and not come on those who would follow. He realized that the sin-and-death cycle which existed had to be broken so that peace could come. Also, he knew that only God could do it.

Verse 6 is more than a rhetorical question. The psalmist poured out his heart in a plea for God to hear him and to grant his request. In Hebrew, the phrase **revive us again** consists of two words. The first is the one that is used several times in Psalm 85; it means *to turn or return*. The second comes from a term that means *to live; to be or become strong, vigorous; or to be restored*. In verse 6, the word means the same but with much more force. The word "again" is not in the Hebrew text, but the idea seems to be present. The Septuagint renders the phrase: "Returning, wilt thou not give us life?" The Latin Vulgate follows this translation. But in the Revised Standard Version "revive" is a valid meaning of the word. The call was for God to raise up the people from their state of death and to restore them. The image is that of spring's return after the winter's death or of grass that revives when rain comes after a long drought. The phrase "that thy people may rejoice in thee" indicates that the psalmist grew hopeful as he presented his petition to God. He knew that the Lord wanted his people to be happy, and nothing else brought gladness to one as did the certainty of a proper relationship with God. Only God's power and grace could do this, and the psalmist prayed confidently for this to become a reality in the nation.

Verses 4-7 again stated a petition that God be kind to the people. In verse 7, the word translated **steadfast love** is the beautiful Hebrew word *(hesedh)* that denotes God's rich and abundant compassion. No English word exists that brings out fully the tenderness of this term. The psalmist laid bare his heart as he pleaded for God's favor and asked for deliverance. He felt that as God's covenant people, the nation had a unique claim on his grace; he called on God to deliver the people from their calamities.

The truism, "Man's extremity is God's opportunity," has been proved many times in personal and national life. One day, Robert Raikes saw a group of little children in the street where many people lived who were employed in manufacturing pins. He expressed his concern to one of the people there. He was told that if he were to pass down that street on a Sunday, he would be shocked to see the crowds of children milling about. Raikes said that, immediately, he determined to make some effort to remedy the situation. His effort resulted in the first Sunday School. From this came a movement which has encircled the globe. God sends his revivals in many ways, but they always are related to human need and implemented by those who have compassionate hearts.

Anticipation of Future Blessings (vv. 8-13)

As Habakkuk did (Hab. 2:1), the psalmist paused to hear God's word. Some interpreters have suggested that verses 1-7 were sung antiphonally, but in verses 8-13 an individual voice spoke. The faithful worshipers received from God the answer that they sought. For a moment, they almost doubted God's salvation; but he intervened to revive and strengthen their faith by his Word. What the psalmist heard in secret, he delivered publicly.

In verse 8, the psalmist became a patient listener who was willing to hear God and to have confidence that what the Lord said would be favorable to the people. The word **peace** meant more than absence of conflict; it meant *a wholesome life that was well rounded and emotionally healthy.*

The words "people" and "saints" (v. 8) come from different terms, but the psalmist probably did not mean any particular contrast by referring to two groups of people. The word **people** conveys the concept of *nations* which was used most frequently of Israel as opposed to the Gentiles. The word **saints** comes from a term that has the idea of kindness or piety. The word in verse 8 means *one who is kind, gracious, merciful, pious, or godly.* The expression "who turn to him in their hearts" literally reads: Let them not turn again to folly.

The Revised Standard Version follows the Septuagint's rendering: "To his saints and to those who turn the heart unto him." The psalmist felt that a great danger existed which would cause the people to return to their former life and forget the punishment which their sins had brought on them.

Verse 9 expanded the result of the peace that God gave. The term **salvation** did not have the restricted sense of future life. Rather, it meant *rescue from all kinds of trouble or danger.* The words expressed confidence that God would intervene in the nation's troubles, and they expressed faith that God would meet individual needs. The glory that had been removed would reside again in the land.

Verses 10-11 described salvation's spiritual aspects. The restored community would reflect God's attributes because it owed its existence to him. The phrase **steadfast love** (v. 10) rendered the Hebrew word *hesedh* of verse 7, while **faithfulness** came from a term that meant *to support, nurse, or bring up.* The best rendering was/is *faithfulness* or *steadiness.* The psalmist saw the blending of two attributes which were opposites in some ways. People were not able to measure up to God's standards and needed his mercy. In a sense, deliverance required both divine grace and human cooperation; but the meaning in verse 10 was that grace abounded to meet human need.

The statement "righteousness and peace will kiss each other" parallels the preceding statement. God demands righteousness; but he also gives peace or well-being as he overlooks people's weaknesses.

The psalmist continued his charming picture of the future. In verse 11, he pictured God's firmness to be like the grass that came upward from the earth; and he depicted ethical conduct coming down from heaven. He did not intend to contrast the way they came; rather, he wanted to emphasize that these spiritual virtues were given the same way as other abundant blessings. God gives spiritual virtues to receptive people.

The word translated "will look down" (see Ps. 14:2) pictures one who bends over or leans forward to look at people and is anxious to provide for them. The rain and sunbeams want to give their blessings; but even more, God wants to send good things to his creation.

Verse 12 dealt with needed temporal blessings. A high standard of national morality brings earthly prosperity. Old Testament writers saw a close connection between virtuous conduct and physical well-being in individual and community life.

In verse 13, the psalmist saw the Lord as a righteous king who was escorted suitably as he went out to begin a new age. Generally, translators have agreed in rendering the first phrase; but the second phrase has presented difficulties. Literally, the Hebrew reads: And maketh his footsteps for a way. In interpreting this statement, one must realize that the passage is poetry; also, one must understand that the Hebrew often states an idea as concisely as possible. With due respect for all other suggestions, the idea seems to be that God's coming to the land in salvation would cause people to walk in his steps.

Some interpreters have seen in verse 13 the prospect that God's coming would cause the people to turn from sin and to be prepared for his appearing. Thus, John the Baptist may have had this passage in mind in his message about Christ.

However we understand verse 13, the psalmist's message is clear. He closed his song by anticipating a time when people would march forward freely. He looked beyond the present to a period of righteousness. He heralded the new day as one in which God's salvation would be evident in the land's prosperity but, even more important, in the people's godly lives.

Lessons for Life from Psalms 12; 14; 80; 85

God's Word stands firm.—In spite of prolonged and severe conflict, the Word of God remains the one authoritative message to people. Blatant unbelief has sought to undermine its message, but God's Word remains fixed forever as the standard for conduct. God's Word is understood better and diffused more widely now than ever. Truly, we should hide it in our hearts so that we might not sin against God. We should wait on the Lord to fulfill his promises.

People usually deny God because they do not want such a

God to exist.—When we accept the fact of God, we also must accept the demands that go with such a belief. When people shut their ears to the voice of duty, they must eliminate God or suffer terrible guilt feelings. We need to keep burning in our hearts the truth that God lives; thus, life has beauty *and* duty.

Nations need God for survival.—Whether we see God as the great Shepherd of his flock or in the Temple with the worshipers, he is the only One who can rescue a decaying society. The nations' ups and downs are connected closely with how they respond to him. When righteous individuals lead and the people follow, great rejoicing comes. However, unless a nation accepts God in its life, judgment will come thoroughly and perhaps quickly. No one can claim to be exempt from the moral laws that God has set up.

Greater ages can come if we meet the conditions.—Just as a person has moral and spiritual obligations, so does a nation. Folly and sin bring misery. People do not have the power to gain God's favor. Only by repentance and trust in God's grace can restoration from sin become a fact.

Personal Learning Activities

1. In Psalm 12, the psalmist was concerned about his nation's _____. (Select the proper response from the list.)
   - (1) Wealth
   - (2) Military might
   - (3) Ruler
   - (4) Sin
2. Psalm 14 expressed great joy because of the large number of righteous people in the world. True____ False____
3. In Psalm 80, the psalmist addressed God as the _____ of Israel. (Choose the proper answer from the list.)
   - (1) King
   - (2) Lord
   - (3) Sovereign
   - (4) Shepherd
4. Psalm 85 was a plea that God (select the correct responses from the list):
   - ____(1) Heal a person
   - ____(2) Restore the nation
   - ____(3) Revive his people
   - ____(4) Give victory

Answers: 1. (4); 2. False; 3. (4); 4. (2), (3).

5 Songs of Faith

Trust in God, which was the Hebrew religion's basic element, dominated Old Testament life. Scripture indicated that God "reckoned" Abraham's faith as righteousness (Gen. 15:6). However, to the patriarch faith meant more than trying to believe in spite of the evidence. He looked on faith as daring to do something in spite of the consequences.

While many psalms breathe confidence in the Lord, a large number gain a distinction because of their function. Most—perhaps all—of Israel's songs found their way into the religious community's worship experiences. They glow in warmth and power because they proclaim a calm and bouyant faith in the face of factors that could shatter life's foundations. Some express the courage and confidence associated with youthful optimism, while others are like rainbows after the flood. One truth is common to all of them: When one refuses to surrender faith, added power comes.

Psalm 16 expresses quiet confidence in the security that comes when one lives constantly in the light of God's presence. Psalm 23 celebrates God's care for the psalmist and the Lord's provision for all his needs. The Psalm expresses his trust in God's never-failing goodness and mercy. Psalm 27 shows implicit faith in God during perilous conditions. Verses 1-6 express the psalmist's confidence because he knew that God was with him. Verses 7-14 lament his being deserted by those closest to him, but they still express certainty that God would not forsake him.

In Psalm 62, the psalmist indicated that hard times had come to him. Friends had turned on him, and he concluded that only God could be trusted. He insisted that brute force and material wealth would disappoint people, but God who has power and steadfast love never will fail.

God Is My Portion (16:1-11)

Psalm 16 reflects all persons' common needs. The expression **Miktam** probably means *one of the "golden" poems*—songs which Israel held to be among David's best works. The Psalm came from a devout and deeply spiritual soul who affirmed his faith when he faced a dangerous situation.

In the first main division (vv. 1-3), the psalmist stated an earnest plea to be preserved because he had put his trust in God. The words formed a general prayer from a confident believer rather than a cry of panic when danger threatened. To the psalmist, the Lord alone could bring happiness. He insisted that no one could enjoy good things apart from a personal relationship with God. He recognized that others also attached themselves to God, and he claimed fellowship with them. They were not rich and powerful people according to the world's estimation, but they were righteous.

Verse 4 may be considered with the preceding verses, or it may be placed apart for special emphasis. With dramatic abruptness, the psalmist turned to those who refused to acknowledge the Lord but took part in worship of idols. He may have referred to foreigners or to his own people who had forsaken their God. He made clear that those who exchanged the true God for false gods increased their grief. He refused to have any part in such worship; he even refrained from speaking words that related to the unacceptable and offensive rituals which were connected with pagan deities.

Verses 5-6 express the psalmist's delight in his background. Like the Israelites who received a desirable piece of land when Joshua allotted property to the tribes, the psalmist knew that God had dealt favorably with him. He had been born in a country that worshiped the true God, and he enjoyed the blessings that came to those who grew up in a favorable environment. Even his longing for spiritual things came because of God's grace.

In verses 7-8, the psalmist pictured the intimate relationship between him and the Lord. God counseled him in the silent watches of the night and disciplined him at his life's deepest level. Because of this, praise swelled in his heart and found expression in song. The psalmist indicated how he responded. He lived in the light of God's presence and always acted as though God were watching him closely. He recognized that God's ever-present help kept him safe and protected him from falling or from being uprooted.

Verses 9-11 climaxed the song. Joy, confidence, and eternal progress came as a result of the fellowship that the psalmist had with his Creator. His heart rejoiced because he knew that he could chant a triumphant song even as he stood on the edge of the grave. He poured out his rapturous faith and testified that fellowship with God abolished death. His spirit embraced the tremendous thought that death is not the final word. Those who live *for* God and *with* God cannot be destroyed. Through God's inspiration, the psalmist was convinced that his joy with God was unending.

The Lord Is My Shepherd (23:1-6)

The Shepherd Provides (vv. 1-2)

The intense tone of Psalm 23 makes clear that the words reflect personal experience. Since many cultures had produced poetry that compared rulers to shepherds, a pastoral people such as Israel would feel compelled to express their relationship with the Lord by such a figure. The psalmist lovingly lingered on the image. Correctly, he drew out the various aspects that were related to the shepherd's care.

The psalmist used the covenant name *Yahweh* to express the One who ministered to his needs. Any other term would have been inadequate. Among a pastoral people, the faithful shepherd was marked by tender care and a watchfulness that did not grow weary. Through the centuries, Israel's God had functioned in this role; he had supplied every need.

The opening statement in verse 1 requires nine English words but only four in Hebrew. Though it is brief, the first phase is full of music, and it falls on the ear like a benediction. Hebrew thought was not abstract; it was concrete and radiantly vivid. The second phrase in verse 1 is the natural and logical conclusion of the opening one. One could catch the spirit of the text even better by translating: Since the Lord is my shepherd, I shall not want.

The word translated **want** came from a term that meant *to lack, be without anything,* or *suffer need.* The psalmist included in his statement everything that could be a proper object of desire, temporal or spiritual, and that pertained to the total person.

In verse 2, the psalmist went back to the sunny days of his youth. He remembered when he enjoyed a carefree life under God's protection as he lay on the meadows like a lamb or rested in a tent by the brook. The form of the two verbs suggested the blending of experience and hope. The psalmist drew together thoughts of the past and the present and projected them into the future to portray a single reflection on God's goodness. The psalmist placed the expression "green pastures" in an emphatic position in the sentence. The word **pastures** meant a dwelling place or habitation and suggested the idea of comfort or satisfaction. The word rendered "green" primarily had nothing to do with color but rather came from a word that meant *to shoot or sprout forth*. The noun meant tender grass or young herbage in contrast to the ripe grass that was ready for mowing. The picture conveyed the calmness and repose of a cool meadow.

The phrase **still waters** also is emphatic and literally means *restful or quiet waters*. The phrase is in contrast to tempestuous and stormy water, and describes gentle and still water with no thought of stagnation. The "still waters" could be a gently running stream and convey the psalmist's thought. The word **lead** primarily means *to conduct* but has in it the idea of sustaining. God gives his people needed rest and provides resources that sustain.

The Shepherd Brings Back (v. 3)

The psalmist added a further image. He pictured God as a wanderer's guide through life. The word translated **restores** meant *to turn or return*. The form that was used conveyed the idea of renewing or refreshing. Especially did it have this meaning when it was used with the term translated "soul." A good translation would be: He causes my life to return or be renewed.

In Hebrew, the word "soul" appears before the term "restores" and refers to the vital energy or spirit. The statement means that God takes one who is exhausted or sad and instills a new dynamic. The idea is not so much that one is wandering or backsliding into sin as it is that the person is weary, troubled, and/or anxious. The Lord reanimates and returns such persons to vigor by encouraging them, exciting them to new effort, and filling their lives with new joy.

Although trouble produced dryness and barrenness in the

soul, God's presence refreshed and strengthened. In the past, he had revealed himself as gracious and merciful. The psalmist knew God would prove to his people that he was able to meet their present and future needs. However, they had to submit to God's guidance which would enable him to bring them back to a place of rest and new motivation.

In verse 3, the word translated **leads** is a different Hebrew term from the one in verse 2. The word in verse 3 means *to guide* but also suggests *to lead back*. Verse 2 affirms that God restores the soul; in verse 3, the meaning seems to be that God leads back into godliness one who has gone astray.

The term **righteousness** comes from a word that primarily means *to be just* or *upright*. The emphasis is on what is right and fair in personal dealings with one's neighbors and acquaintances. The term *straightness* which often is used to translate the word suggests correct conduct in ethical decisions.

The phrase **for his name's sake** (v. 3) literally meant *on account of his name*. Since God had revealed himself as righteous and merciful, he had to prove himself to be consistent and worthy of those attributes. God's nature was at stake; only by acting consistently and in behalf of his people could he vindicate his claim.

The Shepherd Consoles (v. 4)

In verse 4, the psalmist ceased writing *about* the Lord and addressed him. As he thought of his closeness to God through the years, he remembered times of distress and danger. He recalled the trials which he had endured, and he sought to cling to God more ardently because he knew that the Lord had not forsaken him during those perilous times. The phrase "valley of the shadow of death" was a poetical term rather than a literal one. The lovely wording has become such a part of religious vocabulary that one hesitates to interfere with it. However, the expression meant only *deep gloom*; and it was used to express sadness and trouble rather than a departure from the physical world.

The psalmist wrote with confidence; no doubt, he had faced many days of discouragement and sorrow. He had gone through many valleys of deep shadow. In these concrete experiences, he had learned precious lessons about God's protecting and restoring power. The word rendered **evil** carried the idea of *hurtful*. The poet's emphasis was not on the wickedness of the ones who plotted against him but on the hurt that he might suffer because of them. Literally, the psalmist wrote: Thou with me. One who would translate must decide whether to put this in the past, present, or future. Actually, the psalmist meant all three. The same God who had led him to the present point in his life never would forsake him.

The psalmist mentioned two aspects of the shepherd's work which brought comfort and confidence to him. The "rod" served as a weapon of defense. It served as a club with which the shepherd could drive off attacking beasts, and it symbolized the shepherd's office. Since it was bent and crooked at one end, the shepherd used the hook to seize the legs of the sheep that were prone to run away; thus, he kept them with the flock.

The word translated **staff** came from a term that meant *to lean or rest on*. The shepherd not only used it when he was weary but also for assistance in walking. Actually, both words—"rod" and "staff"—could have been translated "staff," which would support the contention of those who insist that only one stick was meant. The psalmist's way of stating his thought, "thy rod and thy staff, they," intensified his feeling of security. Although he dreaded the terrors of the dark valleys, he conquered his fear because he trusted God. He learned that the antidote for his fear was not bold courage but faith in the Shepherd.

The Host Gladdens (v. 5)

Although the figure of speech changed in verse 5, the basic thought was retained. Those who live for God enjoy the blessings of being his guests, even while they march through places where foes lurk and seek to destroy them. In the area where the psalmist lived, a host felt that to ensure a guest's safety was a sacred duty. No intruder could exploit a guest without first conquering the host. The psalmist saw his enemies as those who looked on frustrated and defeated in their evil purpose because they knew that God kept watch over him. The word **enemies** came from a term which meant *to be hostile toward anyone*. Probably, the stronger word *adversary* would render better the meaning. Adversaries sought to distress or vex the psalmist, to bring him discomfort and intense anguish.

The psalmist's picture of a table that was spread in his enemies' sight reflects an even more graphic token of God's care and power than the green pastures (v. 2). He saw life as a journey that exhausts; but, even more, he saw it as a conflict where opponents seek to hurt and destroy. To find sudden refreshment which was spread by an unseen hand that would hold back his foes pictured the ultimate in divine concern.

The word translated "anointest" was not the one for setting aside a king or leader with proper ceremonies. The term referred to unguents and perfumes that were used at an oriental banquet. Hosts customarily performed such acts for their guests at a feast. This type of ointment symbolized joy. The Hebrew verb literally meant *to make fat*, and the term *oil* came from another word which also carried the same idea. The word suggested richness, delicacy, and fertility of the land; the picture was one of abundance and prosperity.

The phrase "my cup runneth over" continued to stress abundance and fullness. The Lord provided much more than the necessities of life. Those who sat at his table had cheerful faces and glad hearts. The generous host treated his guests liberally; he provided to excess.

A Closing Assurance (v. 6)

The psalmist closed with a statement of faith, his testimony of his confidence in a bright future. His memory melted into hope and even anticipation as he looked forward to the days ahead. The word rendered **surely** meant *only* and reflected the deep belief that nothing could defeat a godly person. The phrase "goodness and mercy" was a striking contrast to the fate of the wicked person who constantly was pursued by ruin and faced certain judgment. The divine blessing which had brought sunshine into the psalmist's life promised more, which caused him to sing with growing enthusiasm about God's great riches that were beyond the human mind's power to grasp.

The phrase **all the days of my life** meant *in every varying situation until the psalmist reached the close of life*. Sadness no longer troubled him because his soul had become radiant with God's enlightening presence. The two Hebrew words translated **for ever** literally meant *length of days*. The expression was parallel to the preceding one and meant that God would extend the psalmist's life and make it joyful as long as he resided on earth. He saw that personal and ongoing communion with God was symbolically the same as dwelling in God's house. Eternal life had not been brought to light in Jesus Christ. Only the gospel, climaxed by Christ's resurrection, could enable one to say "always."

The Lord Is My Light and My Salvation (27:1-14)

A Confident Testimony (vv. 1-3)

The psalmist took his stand with courage because he had seen God at work in the past. Since the Lord was with him, he had stood the test in recent struggles and had faced life with assurance and firm faith. He chose light as his first figure of speech because trouble, anxiety, and danger suggest darkness; with God's help, he had come through these victoriously. Although the term *light* was used many times in the Scriptures, the psalmist was the only Old Testament writer who applied the word directly to God.

The word "salvation" primarily denoted deliverance and showed the psalmist's resolve to keep the fires of courage and confidence burning in the face of encamping foes and rising wars. He knew that he could find safety in the Lord's tent and would be lifted above the enemies which surrounded him. Because of this, he refused to be afraid. He expressed both confidence and courage because he knew that God was on his side and was able to protect him from any danger.

The word translated **stronghold** came from a term which meant *to strengthen*. Some scholars have felt that **stronghold** can be rendered best as *fortress* or *refuge* in order to emphasize the psalmist's security in the Lord. However, others have felt that the word *strength* best conveyed the meaning. The term *refuge* would put the emphasis on security against objects of fear or dread. The word *strength* would suggest that God kept the psalmist alive though he (the psalmist) was feeble and easily crushed by trouble and sorrow. Both meanings were present in the psalmist's mind, for he completely depended on God for both security and sustenance.

The two terms translated **fear** and **be afraid** are similar, but the latter Hebrew word seems to be a bit stronger. The first term means *to be anxious*. The latter means *to tremble* and even *to be terrified*. The parallel phrases convey the same thought, but the second seems to be more intense.

In verse 2, the phrase "uttering slanders against me" literally reads: to eat up my flesh. A similar expression occurs in Psalm 15:3, and most interpreters feel that the language is symbolic rather than literal.

Essentially, the words **adversaries** and **foes** mean the same thing. The first means *one who brings distress or adversity and is thus an enemy*. The word **foes** means *one who has enmity toward another*. The name "Job" is a form of this word, which suggests the term *persecuted*.

The form of the words "stumble" and "fall" (v. 2) indicated completed action. Possibly, the psalmist related something that already had occurred which nourished his present confidence. Or, the words might have indicated his certainty that they would take place in the future. The phrase "when evildoers assail me" could be rendered literally: in the drawing near. This leaves indefinite whether or not they had come. Whichever view we take, the psalmist showed faith in God's purpose and power to work for his deliverance.

The confidence that was expressed in verse 3 rested on the Lord's past acts and on the psalmist's present commitment to him. The words "host" and "encamp" came from the same root. One could translate: though a camp encamp against me. The term **war** came from a word which meant *to eat or consume*. The phrase "yet I will" could be rendered: in this I will. This referred primarily to the psalmist's past experience with God but also may have pointed forward to verse 4. No matter how serious the threat might be, the psalmist would trust in God.

A Sincere Desire (vv. 4-6)

Since the psalmist felt certain that God would deliver him from his foes, he set forth his desire for personal fellowship with God. The words "asked" and "dwell" were set side by side to express an ardent longing which had begun in the past, extended into the present, and would reach into the future. Therefore, the psalmist's desire would run throughout his whole life. Whether he meant the Temple or the tabernacle is not the issue. He sought what devout souls in all ages have wanted: the abiding sense of the divine Presence. He referred to the beauty of God's character as manifested in public worship or expressed by symbols that were designed to make those attributes known.

In verse 5, the terms "hide" and "conceal" expressed the confidence that God would protect from dangers in the same way a friendly host would guard his guests. The psalmist drew confidence, courage, and strength from his close fellowship with the Lord which guarded him from fear and a trembling lack of courage. The Hebrew words translated **hide** and **conceal** meant the same, and either one could be translated with either word. Both denoted continuous action: God would go on protecting.

The word **shelter** (v. 5) comes from a term which means *to cover or conceal*. The phrase "cover of his tent" consists of a word for concealment and a term which basically means tent, tabernacle, or dwelling. The words refer to the most private part of God's house or habitation. The language is poetical, not literal; it refers to intimate fellowship with the Lord.

The phrase "upon a rock" (v. 5) comes first in the sentence, followed by a term which means to set up high. One could translate the statement: He will set me up upon a rock. The idea is that God would put the psalmist in a place of security which enemies could not reach.

In verse 6, the word translated "shall be lifted up" is the same term as the one in verse 5 translated "will set me high." The phrase "sacrifices with shouts of joy" is literally *sacrifices of shouting*. But since the word sometimes is used for the sound of a trumpet, some translators have rendered it: sacrifices with trumpet sound. The psalmist repeated himself, but he used two different Hebrew words to express his resolve to sing. The first was a general word for making melody; the second came from a term which meant "to pluck or prune." The second word expressed more fully the overflow of the psalmist's joyful heart. He knew that the life that was hidden with God would know unbounded happiness.

An Urgent Cry (vv. 7-10)

In verse 7, the tone of Psalm 27 changed abruptly. The psalmist wrote as though he felt that God had rejected him. The word "aloud" (v. 7) may have indicated distress that was expressed in audible prayer. The word translated "be gracious" had in it the idea of mercy or compassion and suggested that perhaps the psalmist felt guilt and hesitated to deal with his enemies too hastily. He felt that he had to engage in searching self-criticism and surrender to God's grace.

Translators have difficulty with verse 8 and vary greatly. The literal Hebrew reads: To thee hast said my heart seek my face; thy face Lord I will seek. The basic truth is that the psalmist determined to consult the Lord and repented of the sin that separated him from full fellowship with God. In verses 1-6, the psalmist soared. In the next ones, he became less jubilant. However, he knew that God was consistent and would forgive him when he came to God in sincere faith.

The psalmist gained faith from his decision and claimed divine grace (v. 9). He felt that he deserved free access to God as a friend because he had turned in commitment to the Lord (v. 8). He knew that God acted with integrity and never sent one on a quest which ended in disappointment. The phrase "thou who has been my help" indicated that in times past, God had shown mercy. The psalmist prayed that he had done nothing to forfeit the possibility of present forgiveness. He felt caught-in-a-bind as he realized the pressure that his own conscience had put on him, but he had confidence that God was compassionate. He knew that although he did not face the whim of a divine despot, he must deal with a righteous God. Therefore, he knew that he must submit without reservation; without this attitude, no salvation was possible for him. Thus, he threw himself into God's arms, for he recognized that divine judgment and divine grace blend. The blending of judgment and grace produced the tension which so often occurred in a personal faith encounter with God.

In verse 10, the word "for" probably should be translated *if,* since we have no evidence that the psalmist's parents literally had left him. Some scholars point out that this phrase may be a proverbial expression or idiom that indicated the most forsaken that a person could become. However one interprets verse 10, the meaning is clear. God's love is stronger than that of the closest friend or even human kin.

A Final Appeal (vv. 11-14)

As the psalmist neared the close of his song, he became more specific. Since he had resolved firmly to put his relationship with God in order, he attained inner freedom and outward boldness. Therefore, he confidently asked God to protect him against the violence and lies of those who oppressed him. He repeated his need for guidance but stated clearly that his enemies made such help necessary. The **level path** meant *a straight and smooth one*. Such a path suggested safety; it also was characterized by ethical righteousness.

In verse 12, the word **will** literally meant *soul, spirit,* or *desire*. The "false witnesses" were slanderers who brought untrue charges against the psalmist among the people rather than those who actually had testified in court. The expression "breathe out violence" meant that in meditating constantly on cruel treatment toward the psalmist, the false witnesses were so intense that they panted as they plotted.

Translators have had difficulty with the first phrase in verse 13. An expression was used that can be translated either as an interjection or as a cry with a condition or a qualifier. Some have inserted the words "I had fainted" and rendered the first word "unless": "I had fainted unless I believed to see . . ." (KJV). However, others have insisted that the psalmist was giving a strong affirmation of faith; he was declaring his confidence that the Lord would vindicate him while he still lived on earth. Enemies assailed him, and he was perplexed by his opposition; but he knew that God would deliver him.

Although the psalmist's sky remained dark, he ended his song on a courageous note. In verse 14, he confronted himself; then, he began to hope in God. The faith that the Lord granted him was the kind that did not see but still lived in confident assurance. The psalmist returned to the key with which he began: He recognized that those who trusted God would be conscious of weaknesses but also would be filled with strength. They would be aware of their foes, but they also would be bold to meet them. When the psalmist expressed boldness for the Lord, the result was greater confidence. The word "heart" referred to a person's total personality rather than merely to the emotions.

Psalm 27 moved from faith to fear and back to faith. The psalmist recognized that the key in any relationship with the Lord would be *patience*. He repeated the expression, "Wait for the Lord," because it was fixed deeply in his mind and he wanted to share it with others. He knew that he must do all he could to win life's victories; but in the final sense, God held the key to every problem and difficulty.

J. H. Jowett spoke of the word that the psalmist used for "wait" as signifying something that twined itself like ivy around an oak or a little child with his arms drawn tightly around his mother's neck. He also said: "To wait on the Lord is to make the Lord the clinging place of the soul, and therefore the resting place, and therefore the growing place."[1] The poet wrote correctly:

> How difficult the task to wait
> For promises to be fulfilled.[2]

I Wait for God (62:1-12)

Through distress and pain, the psalmist learned that only God gave a haven from the storms which affected life. The events that were connected with Absalom's revolt would be a fitting context for Psalm 62. The Psalm's basic thrust was that only God met the needs of troubled souls. Everything else disappointed people and could not meet their needs.

In verses 1-2, the psalmist stated a strong affirmation of faith in God as his only hope. In verses 3-4, he described his enemies and their designs; and he addressed them with indignation. He accused them of devising mischief and seeking to cast people down from their high places. He blasted them for their malice and hypocrisy, and he claimed that they delighted in falsehood and pretended to be friends while they were utterly false in heart.

In verses 5-7, the psalmist reaffirmed his confidence in God by repeating his words in verses 1-2. He concluded by declaring that his salvation and glory were not at the disposal of people but rested on God. In verses 8-12, he urged others to trust in God (vv. 8-10) and gave reasons why they could do so with confidence (vv. 11-12).

Psalm 62 proved that the psalmist's wrestling with the Lord was a glorious testimony to the true spirit of prayer. He turned away from meditating in silence and focused his attention on God. When he centered his thoughts on God, a stillness came to

his soul. From a sense of not knowing where to turn in his anxiety, the psalmist moved to a firm footing so that he no longer wavered. He attained peace of mind and sound judgment on which he could rely.

Lessons for Life from Psalms 16; 23; 27; 62

Without God, life is meaningless.—Until people have met the Lord and surrendered to him, they begin at no beginning and work toward no end. Everyone wants to enjoy a full and rich life. However, without the Lord people constantly are working and finding no lasting satisfaction and fulfillment.

God gives what his people need.—When God's people pray for his will to be done in their lives, they also are asking him to supply the things that he knows are necessary to bring them happiness. God would be unfair to his people if he gave everything for which they ask. He gives the things that will enrich them and help them to realize their potential.

If God is with his people, what else matters?—Believers may be sure that nothing can oppose them successfully when they are linked with the Lord. He is a better and more faithful friend than anyone else, and he will not leave his own exposed to things or people that will bring harm.

Though others fail, God never will.—When people resolve to believe and follow the Lord completely, they can face the future with confidence. Defeatism should be absent from the Christians' vocabularies. Believers can be confident without being cocksure. Think of everything terrifying that this world can produce. Nothing in the list can separate God's people from his protecting hand. He never disappoints his own or refuses to help them.

---

1. James Hastings, ed., "Psalms," *The Speaker's Bible* (Aberdeen, Scotland: The "Speakers' Bible" Offices, 1925), II:192.
2. *Ibid.*, p. 193.

Personal Learning Activities

1. According to Fred Wood, Psalm 16 reflects the belief that fellowship with God (choose the correct answer from the list):
   ____(1) Is a burden ____(3) Abolishes death
   ____(2) Is useless ____(4) Is broken easily
2. In Fred Wood's interpretation of Psalm 23, God was pictured as _____ and _____. (Select the proper responses from the list.)
   (1) Judge (3) King
   (2) Shepherd (4) Host
3. The psalmist who wrote Psalm 27 was the only Old Testament writer to apply the word *light* directly to God. True____ False____
4. In Psalm 27, the psalmist concluded his song with a call for _____. (Choose the correct answer from the list.)
   (1) Courage (3) Love
   (2) Patience (4) Kindness
5. Psalm 62 asserted that only a person's own resources provided a haven in life's storms. True____ False____

Answers: 1. (3); 2. (2), (4); 3. True; 4. (2); 5. False.

6 Songs of Personal Anguish

Psalms 22; 42—43; 51; 109

Those who have preached to, taught, or written to sufferers always have been needed because, as Tennyson wrote: "Never morning wore to evening, but some heart did break."[1] In Israel, national crisis called for a public fast; private grief caused individuals to pour out their hearts to God in secret petition. On both occasions, authors produced literature that reflected the pain. To a large extent, the psalms that were related to individual suffering dealt with loneliness which always has been a major result of a broken heart. The psalmists stressed their complete dependence on God. Though they began with cries of anguish, they never failed to express triumphant faith before they ended their recorded prayers.

The selected poems that represent personal anguish were from people who were anxious, perplexed, and hurting. Psalm 22 expressed isolation and agony. No doubt, Jesus had the Psalm in mind as he hung on the cross. He framed his cry of loneliness from the opening words of Psalm 22. Psalms 42—43 actually made up one song. Likely, the psalmist was away from the Temple and unable to go to it. He felt removed from God and ridiculed because of his faith, and he longed for God's presence. Nevertheless, he ended his song by affirming his hope in God. Psalm 51 was a cry for pardon. Psalm 109 was a prayer, but it contained an angry plea. This Psalm expressed rage as the psalmist lashed out against those who oppressed him.

My God, My God, Why? (22:1-31)

Psalm 22 opened with the words that Jesus used centuries later to express his soul's anguish. It moved from misery's lowest depths to the greatest heights of assurance. Verses 1-19 dealt with the psalmist's suffering as he came to the grave's brink and knew utter despair. In verses 20-31, the despair passed as he expressed confidence concerning the future. The Psalm's main thrust consisted of these two themes.

In the first section (vv. 1-5), the psalmist described his sufferings and pleaded for deliverance. He appealed to God's character and the mercy that he had experienced in past days. Next (vv. 6-21), he pictured himself as the victim of persecutors although he had depended on God all of his life. In verse 11, he made an urgent plea, while in successive verses he described his plight. The section closed with another prayer for deliverance.

The psalmist suddenly changed his outlook. Darkness and despair passed as he looked forward with confidence to the future. After a prayer for help in verses 20-21, his hope for the future dominated the poem. Beginning with verse 22, he thanked God for answered prayer and vowed to give testimony

and praise because God looked with mercy on him. Each verse took on greater intensity as the psalmist rose in praise and power. The Psalm closed with a picture of the world's conversion when people who were not yet alive would serve and praise God.

Five times (vv. 1,7,8,16,18), the psalmist penned words that were picked up by the Gospel writers in connection with Jesus' death. The moving pathos in Psalm 22 argues strongly that it reflects an individual's personal experience. However, many features appeared to transcend the limits endured by one person. Therefore, some scholars have seen in the speaker the ideal righteous sufferer. Others have applied it to the people of national Israel who suffered for their faith.

Longing for God (42:1 to 43:5)

Yearning Because of Past Memories (vv. 1-5)

The psalmist opened his song by expressing his intense desire for fellowship with God. The word rendered "hart" (v. 1) indicated a female deer. The timorous hind was a fitting symbol for the psalmist's soul. The term **longs** suggested the sufferings of wild animals in a prolonged drought. The word meant to look up toward anything or to yearn for it. Pictured was the hind's intense desire for water during the hottest part of the day. The "flowing streams" were waterbrooks that ran in the valley.

Through his song, the psalmist expressed his deep longing for a closer relationship with God. Then centuries later, Christians began to express that same desire. Through the years, they have continued to long for more intimate experiences of God's presence in their lives. Bernard of Clairvaus expressed that deep desire when he wrote:

> Jesus, the very thought of Thee
> With sweetness fills my breast;
> But sweeter far Thy face to see,
> And in Thy presence rest.

When the psalmist used a hind's thirst to express his longing for a deeper sense of God's presence, he chose a vivid comparison. A timid deer that was fearful of attack offered a striking illustration. The psalmist was hunted by his enemies and felt that he could not live without spiritual refreshment from worship. In the withering heat, water was precious; in fact, life was impossible without it. God's presence was just as essential for life as water; thus, the word "living" (v. 2) was used to describe God because without the Lord nothing mattered. The psalmist felt that death meant a state of existence without God.

The expression "behold the face of God" was a technical phrase for a pilgrimage to the Temple. The psalmist asked when the privilege of uniting with his people in public prayer and praise would be restored. This longing was even more painful because at that time, he was living in a pagan land.

The psalmist's heavy heart had driven from him all desire to eat. The word translated **tears** (v. 3) literally meant *weeping*. Instead of eating food, he had wept. Excessive sorrow had taken away his appetite so that he no longer relished food. To aggravate his grief and sharpen his frustration, enemies had taunted him and had demanded that he show proof of his God's presence.

All four verbs in verse 4 suggested continuous action. The psalmist gave free course to his feelings as he thought of the past. In exile, he continued to recall the happy scene of former days. The form of the word "went" suggested that his custom had been to conduct pilgrimages for the festivals. He did this regularly. He did not cling to the past as a luxury of grief or indulge in the recollection because a "'sorrow's crown of sorrow is remembering happier things.'"[2] Rather, he felt that retrospect was the best antidote to the heathens' sneers. He knew that the God in whose service he once found such delight could not have deserted him.

The word translated **pour out** meant *to melt* or *dissolve* when it was applied to grief, or *to overflow* when it was related to joy. The psalmist's emotions went back and forth from agony to ecstasy as he thought of other days. The word translated **throng** denoted a thicket of trees or thick woods, and from this it came to mean *a crowd of men*.

During the brief time when the bitter present ceased to exist for the psalmist, he saw himself with a group expressing joy and praise. The phrases "glad shouts" and "songs of thanksgiving" (v. 4) suggested chanting hymns to God. The word **multitude** came from a term which meant *to be turbulent* or *to rage* when it was applied to a tumultuous crowd. Thus, the noun meant *noise, sound, multitude* and suggested the idea of singing. The phrase **keeping festival** came from a term which meant *to dance;* in some cases, it meant *to reel* or *to be giddy.* From this came the idea *to keep* or *celebrate a feast,* since this was done by leaping and dancing. The psalmist looked back with joy at times when he had engaged in this activity. No doubt, he also looked forward to taking part in such worship again.

Verse 5 contains a refrain which appeared two other times (42:11; 43:5). On this literary basis, scholars have insisted that the two Psalms originally were one; they have divided the one poem into three stanzas. In this refrain, the psalmist's truer self chided the weaker self for its despondency and complaint. He sought to comfort and to encourage himself by letting his stronger and more valiant part speak to the discouraged element of his personality.

The form of the word translated "cast own" (v. 5) suggested continuous action. Also, the psalmist used a form which implied that he realized he was "doing it to himself." The literal meaning of the term translated **cast down** meant *to bow, to be brought low,* or *to be depressed—to sink down under the weight of sorrow.* The Septuagint translated the question: "Why art thou grieved?" The psalmist said to himself that he really had no reason to be depressed. He knew that he cherished his grief improperly. The word "disquieted" also conveyed continuous action. It meant *to be agitated, troubled,* or *anxious in mind* as though one moaned internally.

The form of the word "hope" indicated the psalmist's strong command to himself. He knew that he needed to wait for God to intervene in his crisis. The word translated **shall . . . praise** came from a term that meant *to throw or cast.* The form in verse 5 meant *to confess openly,* thus *to give thanks* or *to praise.* The form has a future thrust in this context but also suggests continual activity. The psalmist looked forward to praising God many times in the future.

The phrase "my help and my God" appears in some versions as the "the help of his countenance" (KJV) which is a literal rendering of the text. The term **help** comes from a word which means *to deliver, save,* or *set free.* This word is followed in the Hebrew text by the noun countenance or face. The text may be rendered "salvation of his face" or his presence.

As the psalmist recalled happier and hallowed hours, he drew on the resources that he had through his relationship with God. He realized that too much looking at himself could lead to self-pity and threaten his communion with the Lord. Briefly, he reached the point where he saw a way open which could lead him beyond suffering and distress. In a touching dialogue with his soul, he realized that one was not helped by weeping and grieving. He saw that this only made suffering worse, so he resolved to wait for God. He trusted that his guilt would lead him from darkness into light.

Depression Because of Present Adversity (vv. 6-11)

Though the psalmist spoke comfort to his heart, he could not banish all of the gloom that filled it. The break in the clouds lasted only a moment, then gray filled the sky once more. The hopefulness that was expressed in the refrain which ended the first stanza passed away, and the psalmist admitted his depression. The form of the verb translated "cast down" (v. 6) suggests that he brought about his own condition by being unable to cope with being beyond the frontiers of Zion.

Sadness flooded the psalmist's soul. His sorrow was made even more bitter because he was in a foreign land. Homesickness caused heart pains as he spoke of his location. The "land of Jordan" (v. 6) was east of the river, and "Hermon" was in the northeast part of Palestine. The psalmist used the plural, Hermons, probably because several summits made up the mountain range. Likely, the place that was indicated was in the Hermon area on a lower peak named **Mizar** that has not been located with certainty. The word meant *little mountain* and may have been a secluded place where the psalmist lived while he was in exile.

The word translated **deep** (v. 7) meant *a mass of water* or *a flood*. The word "calls" suggested the picture of the waves speaking or responding to one another as they flowed southward. The melting snows on Mount Hermon formed thunderous waterfalls, and the scenery suggested to the psalmist the troubles that had descended on him.

Faith swelled up within the psalmist, however, and confidence returned. He felt that soon he would know God's favor again and would express thanks for the Lord's goodness. He reached out to take hold of a hand that chastened him; he showed his trust as he clung to the One whom he feared was forsaking him. He knew that God directed the mighty flow of waters around him, and he deepened his conviction that the flood of troubles which threatened him would not drown him.

The words "day" and "night" (v. 8) suggested that the psalmist viewed God's love as remaining constant, though a momentary situation might cause things to seem otherwise. The term translated "steadfast love" was the Hebrew word *hesedh* which Old Testament writers used to express the highest concept of God's mercy that they knew. The term **commands** meant *to constitute, appoint, and determine or decree*. The form in verse 8 gave extra emphasis to the action: God decreed or appointed steadfast love for the psalmist. The basic idea of the Hebrew word rendered **prayer** was *mediation* or *intercession*; it indicated a provision that enabled people to communicate with God and to express their religious feelings and longings.

After recalling God's past mercy and expressing his own present faith, the psalmist complained once more because he felt that God had left him and had exposed him to evil men's sneers. He felt that God's apathy, which gave the psalmist's enemies cause to blaspheme, was unfair. Conflicting emotions stirred in him because he felt that God should have been his defense and helper rather than one who exposed him to suffering.

The phrase **deadly wound** (v. 10) expressed the psalmist's severe feeling. The word rendered **body** also could be rendered *bone*. One interesting translation of the entire phrase is "a sword in my bones" (KJV). The psalmist's enemies inflicted severe pain on him; their taunts cut him like a knife.

The psalmist faced double jeopardy because he doubted God and was forced to endure his enemies' scornful questions which reinforced his doubt. The question thrown at him implied that if God existed, he either could not aid those who trusted him or was dissatisfied with the psalmist and refused to help.

The struggle produced another refrain. The psalmist returned to God with trust. His faith struggled with fear but always had the last word. He refused to let God go until he received God's blessing. As before, this refrain contained self-reproof and self-exhortation. The psalmist came to the firm conviction that he ought not to be depressed and to feel rejected. He exhorted himself and expressed assurance that he would be permitted to praise God once more.

Confidence Because of Future Hope (43:1-5)

The psalmist's struggle against the doubts which had seized him ended in victory. He reached the state in which he passed triumphantly through the darkness to confidence that his prayer had been granted. The word translated **vindicate** (v. 1) usually is rendered "judge," but in the context of verse 1 it means *to undertake one's cause, interpose in his behalf, or do* *justice in the case.* The psalmist knew he had been wronged and urged God to show to all people that he (the psalmist) was not guilty of his insolent foes' charges.

The phrase "ungodly people" literally reads: people not compassionate. Once more the vivid term *hesedh* was used; it expressed deep affection and tender mercy: Those who opposed the psalmist had no mercy. The reference could have been to Absalom, David's son, who fomented the rebellion that may have served as the context for Psalm 43.

In verse 2, the psalmist's plea arose from his faith and an ardent desire that God's righteousness would be revealed. His prayer was not motivated by any legal claim on God. He felt that God's righteousness was at stake rather than his own revenge. He realized that God's righteousness did not always accord with what a person thought it was, but he boldly asked God to show his power so that all people would see his true character. The phrase "cast me off" literally reads: rejected. The word is in contrast to the term in 42:9 translated "forgotten." Since the psalmist had received no answer to his previous prayer, he began to feel not only that God had forgotten him but that God had refused him. The question, "Why go I mourning?" differs slightly in the Hebrew from the one in the previous refrain (42:9) but conveys essentially the same meaning. The form is a bit more emphatic, and some suggest that the expression in verse 2 is rendered best: walk about by myself.

Though he was discouraged, the psalmist boldly presented his claim once more. In beautiful, heartfelt phrases, he came close to personifying God's blessings for which he prayed. In the context of verse 3, the word "light" was equivalent to *favor* or *mercy*, as when one prayed for the light of God's presence. The word "truth" suggested God's faithfulness.

The psalmist prayed that God would be consistent in character by restoring to him the privileges and blessings from which he had been driven unjustly. The psalmist's gloomier mood had run its course; his grief, which could find no fresh words, began to dry up. After he had repeated his complaints mechanically, their cessation became near. He could find nothing new to say; thus, he began the road back to faith.

The "holy hill" (v. 3) was Mount Zion where God was worshiped. The "dwelling" was the sacred tent which was regarded as the Lord's abode.

Verse 4 showed that the psalmist had won the struggle; then, the rage in his soul had calmed down. He looked forward to communing with God again in worship. He wrote of his ultimate goal as though he was sure that he would realize it. The "altar of God" was the place where sacrifices were offered, and the psalmist felt certain that he would unite with others again in public worship of God. The "lyre" was the harp, a common instrument in that day. To us, the phrase "O God, my God" seems a bit awkward, but it appears in some psalms where the divine name is *Elohim* rather than *Yahweh*. The repetition suggested that the psalmist thought of his God not in a general sense but in a particular one. His God was a Person to whom the psalmist had devoted himself and whom he regarded as his companion even in affliction and trouble.

The refrain that closed Psalm 42 occurs once more with no new thought, but it is intensified by its repetition. No relapse into sadness follows the words. The psalmist's faith had a long struggle with uncertainty, but trust and assurance had the last word as he conquered his fear. His melancholy recollection became for him a joyful hope!

Plea for Forgiveness (51:1-19)

A Poignant Plea for Pardon (vv. 1-6)
Sin crushed the psalmist's heart and caused him to see his great guilt. He made no attempt to excuse his wicked conduct or to plead extenuating circumstances. Deep and dreadful remembrance of his crime made him stretch out his hands toward God and implore for unmerited love and favor—the true definition of grace. Scholars agree that only one incident in David's life could serve as the background for this poem: his sin with Bathsheba (2 Sam. 11:1-26).

In verses 1-2, David used three words to express his wrongdoing. The word **transgressions** came from a term that meant *to revolt or rebel*. The verb signified a sharp break, a defiance of authority, or an entering into territory where one should not trespass. The term **iniquity** suggested *crookedness, perversion, or twisted attitude and conduct;* it also included the guilt associated with the action. The word **sin** suggested *missing the mark or falling short of one's goal in life*. David stood fully exposed before God, guilty on all three counts.

David also described the removal of guilt in a threefold picture. The words "blot out" expressed sin as a debt that was recorded in God's book which needed to be erased and canceled. The term "washed" implied far more than the external dirt that was removed by the fuller's process or the ceremonial function which the term often signified. David's guilt required a removal of inward filth that haunted his soul. The word "cleanse" suggested that David's brightness and splendor had been covered by the awfulness of his sin. He needed to be declared or pronounced pure, and only God could do it! The two sets of three which David used testified eloquently that he was broken down under the weight of his guilt. Because he took God seriously, he felt deeply about that which separated him from the Lord's presence.

In verse 3, David made the phrases "my transgressions" and "my sin" emphatic. Also, he made the first person pronoun "I" emphatic. He made no efforts to conceal his misdeeds. His words revealed more than the fleeting mood of a depressed conscience. Shocked by the knowledge that he had defied God's laws, he expressed clearly that he was conscious of his personal responsibility.

David shut out all other aspects of his guilt as he viewed it in the light of his relationship to God. Of course, he had sinned against others; but when these side issues were compared to his guilt before God, they faded into insignificance. He shared the common view of the Old Testament leaders who understood the true nature of sin. In its ultimate nature, all sin was against God because he alone created persons and the moral standard. David added to this thought by stating clearly that God had every right to bring the results of one's misdeeds on the sinner. In doing so, God acted consistently with his nature.

In verse 5, David went deeper in his appeal to God. He stated that he (David) shared every person's proneness to sin. He did not indicate that the act which resulted in his being conceived was sinful. Also, he was not stating the idea of original sin. He was born into a context where evil was real and prevalent. He emphasized his heart's deep depravity; however, he did not state this to excuse himself. He wanted to stress his need for God's pardon and to urge the Lord to show mercy. In the Hebrew text, the phrases "in iniquity" and "in sin" were made emphatic. David knew that he could not provide his own cleansing. He was driven to God because he knew that he must find help from the Lord or sink into despair.

David made clear that the Lord insisted on a person's being perfectly sincere with himself, his associates, and with God.

The phrase **inward being** (v. 6) meant *the inward parts* or *the reins*—the most secret place of a person's thought and will that others did not see but which God knew. God demanded that a person be inwardly what he or she appeared to be outwardly. Any wisdom that one had must have its origin at that point: in the inward being. Truth went to the deepest part of one's being and exposed the most secret thoughts and purposes. Advanced religious knowledge could not come by one's clever thoughts but by insight into ultimate truth that God would grant only to those whose motives were unmixed.

A Passionate Prayer for Purity (vv. 7-12)

Beginning with verse 7, Psalm 51 stresses personal purity within rather than pardon from guilt. Of course, both ideas are present in both sections; but the poem seems to be divided at this point.

One who was defiled by contact with a dead body became clean by using hyssop. However, David recognized that he needed more than ceremonial rites to restore his broken spiritual health to joyous vitality.

David knew that he needed a personal touch—a spiritual transformation that would lift him from the depths of depression and give him the joy which he once had known. He appealed to God to serve as Priest and remove all that defiled him. The word "wash" (v. 7) was used often in the Scriptures and was the same term that was used in verse 2. It described the fuller who removed the defiling stains from dirty garments. David prayed for inner renewal, to be white as snow. This natural emblem of purity contrasted with the scarlet of sin that was suggested by the blood-stained hands in verse 14.

The ritually cleansed person once more shared in the privileges that went with religious worship. David compared the divinely pardoned sinner with such a one; he urged God to cause him to receive the privileges that produced ecstasy and delight. When he found that the barrier which prevented his communion with God was removed, he heard a sweet voice from heaven which spoke peace. The phrase "bones which thou hast broken" (v. 8) was an idiom which expressed the deep sorrow and pain of a troubled conscience. The word "broken" (crushed) probably should have been translated *shattered*. The word "bones" actually stood for the whole personality. David did not allude so much to a physical malady as to his soul's depression that was brought about by his recognition that he

...ntinually felt that God gazed on him in displeasure. ...ed an unusual expression when he asked God to hide his (God's) face, since this usually indicated a withdrawal of God's favor. However, by this request David asked God to turn away from looking at his wrongdoing. A common expression for atonement was that God covered over sin so that he no longer saw it. With the word translated "blot out," David prayed for God to take away anything that was recorded against him. He wanted everything that testified of his sin erased, canceled, and destroyed.

Verses 10-12 contain six prayers that breathe the spiritual and evangelical spirit which is found in the New Testament. They rank among the highest peaks of Old Testament revelation. When David asked God to create for him a clean heart, he used the same word that was used in the creation story. The term meant to bring into being something that did not exist previously. David did not pray for God to restore what had been; rather, he pleaded for a radical change to take place that would make him a transformed person.

The word translated **in** (v. 10) actually meant *for*; David asked God to do what he never could attain in his own strength. This petition sprang from David's realization that sin was ingrained deeply in him and that transformation was not self-achieved but was God's gift.

The phrase **new and right** translates a word which means *to be upright, sincere, true, prepared, or ready.* Many translators prefer the translation "steadfast" and suggest that David prayed for a spirit which would stand firm in the moment of temptation. He asked for strength to be fixed and resolute in his allegiance to God, unmoved by the assaults of temptation. He knew that a holy life could come only from God's creative power which could make him constant in spirit and consistent in character.

In verse 11, David prayed that God would not exclude him from divine favor. The expression "thy holy spirit" could be rendered literally: spirit of thy holiness. It was mentioned only one other time in the Old Testament (Isa. 63:10-11). This phrase prepared the way for the New Testament teaching of the Holy Spirit, a member of the Godhead.

In Psalm 51:12, the Hebrew could be rendered literally: cause to return to me. This suggested that sin had destroyed the assurance of God's help which always was a cause to rejoice.

David expressed confidence as he prayed for the deliverance which he knew God could and would grant him. In former days, David had known the happiness that came when he was God's friend; but because he had sinned, he had lost his peace of mind. His sad and cheerless soul longed for comforting evidence that only his fellowship with God, not his relationship to the Lord, was severed.

David also asked that God give him an attitude that would respond freely to the right things. He desired to be eager in service, quick in obedience, and spontaneous in response to God's slightest wishes. The word translated **willing** meant *voluntary, ready,* or *prompt.* A further derived meaning was *liberal, generous,* or *noble-minded.* In reality, David prayed for grace and strength that would cause him to be ready always to do God's commandments. Delitzsch wrote: "What is meant is . . . the human spirit made free from the dominion of sin by the Holy Spirit, to which good has become an inward, as it were instinctive, necessity."[3] David wanted to be kept from falling by a divine inspiration that would cause him to think and do spontaneously what God approved.

A Persistent Promise to Praise (vv. 13-19)

David felt that the future relief and happiness would move him into a more expansive mood. He knew that a conscience set free from guilt and a heart renewed by God's Spirit could not keep silent. He vowed to become an evangelist with a heart full of thanksgiving for God's grace and mercy. God's pardon would produce in him such a strong feeling that he would be compelled to tell others about his experience and to urge them to follow his example. The word **teach** (v. 13) meant *to instruct or train.*

In verse 14, the word translated **deliver** meant *to separate or rescue.* The phrase **blood guiltiness** meant both bloodshed and the guilt for such an action. The plural form of the word suggested blood that was spilled in violence. David knew that he had committed a terrible deed, and the guilt of it continued to haunt him.

The word **salvation** (v. 14) comes from a term that primarily means *to be rich, liberal,* or *noble.* From this comes the idea *to be freed* and also the meaning of *deliverance.* The emphasis is on God's abundant resources which David knew existed nowhere else.

The phrase **sing aloud** (v. 14) basically means *to shout for joy,* *to celebrate* or *praise*. The term **deliverance** means *to be declared righteous* or *justified*, thus *to be freed from sin*. David would celebrate God's forgiving him.

In verse 15, the word "Lord" was not a translation of the covenant word *Yahweh*. David did not use that word in the entire poem, probably because he keenly felt the breach of fellowship that sin had caused. The use of this word for Lord, however, would suggest that he felt nearer to God than when he began the poem. In the Hebrew text, the phrase "open thou my lips" may be rendered: Lord, thou will open my lips. The next phrase gave the result of that action.

In verse 16, David did not repudiate sacrificial worship; rather, he meant that God would not accept ritual as a substitute for repentance. The term **sacrifice** came from a word which meant *to slay*, especially in ritualistic performance. The word described any sacrifice that was made by blood, but such sacrifices were distinguished from the burnt offering which was not eaten. The term applied to sin offerings, trespass offerings, or thank offerings and stood opposed to those that were made without blood.

The term rendered **burnt offering** came from a word that meant *to go up* or *ascend*. The sacrifice that this word described was consumed totally or made to ascend on the altar. The offering was voluntary and showed the people's zeal to comply with religion's external forms. The word **delight** came from a term which meant *to be favorably disposed toward anyone* or *anything*. The term **pleased** came from a word which meant *to accept kindly* or *graciously*. David used the verb in its technical sense; he meant that God would not accept a burnt offering as the price of forgiveness. He wrote as one who had seen the hidden relationships of his life; therefore, he could not try to attain God's favor by material gifts and outward acts.

In verse 17, the words "spirit" and "heart" both have the idea of total personality. Although David added the term "contrite" in the second line, the two statements are parallel. The word **broken** meant *torn* or *shattered*, while the term **contrite** meant *bruised* or *crushed*. David knew that the joy which came from forgiveness did not banish sorrow and contrition for wrongdoing. He realized that his heart had to have a deep sense of sin even after pardon came.

David's humility reflected more than his momentary state of mind. He knew that repentance had to become a daily attitude. He came to a far-reaching transformation in his view of sacrifice. A person had to see that God demanded one's self-will and self-importance be renounced in self-surrender to God.

In verses 18-19, David turned from himself and his deep sorrow to think of God's holy city and to pray for it. He did not want his misconduct to hinder God's cause in the world. He prayed for the city's walls to be built the first time, not repaired or restored. Verse 18 could be a statement of what God would do rather than a prayer for him to do it.

Verses 18-19 seem to be the climax to the Psalm. To David, religious forms, institutions, and ceremonies still were necessary. Since he intended for Psalm 51 to be used in worship, he concluded by recognizing the value of form and ceremony in the religious community's life. He knew that spirit was more important than ritual, but he saw no inconsistency in combining the two.

Prayer for Vengeance (109:1-31)

Ruthless and godless people hurled groundless accusations against the psalmist who wrote Psalm 109, although he had dealt with them in love. He felt that he must pray for them; and in the tense situation, he cried to God. At first, he found it difficult to intercede for his enemies because his soul was too heavy

with their harsh charges. Before he swore to his own innocence, he called on God in his own behalf.

Verses 1-5 contain the psalmist's appeal for help against the merciless enemies that sought to ruin him by false charges and treacherous slanders. Their hostility was without cause. Worse than that, these malicious enemies returned evil for good, hate for love. The foes were described as deceitful and lying; in their fighting and making false charges, they used words of hatred for no reason. The context suggested that at one time, the persons referred to had been connected closely with the psalmist and had received benefits from him.

In verses 6-20, the psalmist broke out into an emotion-charged prayer that God would act for him by judging his oppressors. He referred particularly to one person who had been prominent in afflicting him or instigating others. He wanted the man's family to be destitute. The words have caused Christians difficulty because the tone was bitter and vindictive.

The best explanation for the psalmist's words and tone is that the Old Testament is not the New Testament and does not represent mature Christian standards. In the full light of the gospel, we see that such prayers never have had God's approval. However, the psalmist belonged to his own day and wrote according to his understanding and his people's ability to comprehend. His expressions make Christians thankful that they live under the law of love. The statements set an example of moral earnestness, righteous indignation, and burning zeal for God's cause and for justice. In this sense, Psalm 109 and others like it can be accepted as inspired.

Beginning with verse 21, the psalmist turned to beg for God's mercy on him. He recognized his weakness and pointed out that his accusers scorned him without mercy. In verses 28-29, he returned briefly to his request that his enemies be punished. Verses 30-31 close the Psalm. The psalmist repeated his prayer for himself and ended with calm assurance that his suffering almost was completed.

Lessons for Life from Psalms 22; 42—43; 51; 109

God knows when his people suffer.—Although his people often feel alone in their grief, they must trust the One who promised: "'I will not leave you desolate'" (John 14:18).

Since life is brief, people need to make the most of it.—Some things are more important than others, and people need to choose wisely. Most of all, however, an intimate fellowship with God should head the list of their priorities.

Only God is sufficient for life's crises.—People need patience because the Lord meets their needs only when he knows that the time is right. To do God's will gives resources from which they can draw when they are discouraged.

All people need God.—Something deep within causes people to cry out for fellowship with the divine Creator. Augustine said: "Thou madest us for Thyself, and our heart is restless, until it repose in Thee."[4]

Sin is terrible, but God's grace is greater than people's guilt.—Nothing causes persons as much grief as the knowledge that they have transgressed God's law. Only the assurance of divine forgiveness can make them become new persons.

Only in Jesus can people rise above their human selfishness and immature attitudes.—Individuals find that to show a spirit of love toward those who mistreat them is difficult, almost impossible. Believers must grow in Christ before they can reach the goal of praying *for* rather than *against* those who despitefully use them and persecute them.

1. Alfred L. Tennyson, "In Memoriam," VI, stanza 2.

2. A. F. Kirkpatrick, *The Book of Psalms* (New York: Cambridge University Press, 1900), II and III:229.

3. C. F. Keil and F. Delitzseh, "Psalms," *Commentary on the Old Testament* (Grand Rapids: William B. Eerdmans Pub. Co., 1976), V:140.

4. Stanley Irving Stuber, compiler and ed., *The Christian Reader: Inspirational and Devotional Classics* (New York: Association Press, 1952), p. 70.

Personal Learning Activities

1. Psalm 22 has held a special attraction because some of its words were used in connection with (select the proper response from the list):

   ____(1) King David   ____(3) Jesus' death
   ____(2) Temple worship   ____(4) The prophet Jeremiah

2. In Psalm 42, the psalmist expressed his longing for _____. (Choose the correct answer from the list.)

   (1) Peace   (3) God
   (2) Happiness   (4) Rest

3. In Psalms 42—43, the psalmist exhorted himself to _____. (Select the proper answer from the list.)

   (1) Seek help from others   (3) Give up
   (2) Hope in God   (4) Make greater effort

4. Psalm 51 was a throbbing plea for (choose the correct responses from the list):

   ____(1) Cleansing   ____(3) Restoration
   ____(2) Forgiveness   ____(4) A willing spirit

5. Psalms of vengence, such as Psalm 109, indicate the ancient Israelites' burning concern for justice. True ____ False ____

Answers: 1. (3); 2. (3); 3. (2); 4. (1), (2), (3), (4); 5. True.

7 Songs of Praise to the King of Glory

Most Hebrew Psalms began as a part of the worshiping congregation, or they soon became such. They represented a broad area of Israel's religious life. Though some belonged solely to the general praise format, others dealt specifically with tribute to God as King.

Psalm 24 celebrates God's sovereignty over the earth and the people in it. It states God's demand for personal righteousness and describes his majesty as the King of glory.

Psalm 103 joyfully celebrates God's restoring the psalmist. It deals with the Lord's forgiveness, redemption, steadfast love, and mercy. One major section (vv. 10-18) reminds others of spiritual blessings that they had received from God.

Psalm 121 answered a universal and timeless question: Where do people find effective and sufficient help? The psalmist contended that the Lord who created heaven and earth had been, and still was, powerful and alert to keep his people.

Psalm 139 was written from deep personal experience with God; it stated the conviction that God always was present. The psalmist concluded his remarkable confession with the request that God look into him and do what was necessary to guarantee that their fellowship would remain.

Who Is the King of Glory? (24:1-10)

Psalm 24 contains three clearly marked sections; each differs from the others in style and subject matter. The Psalm has a basic unity, and the variety in style is not any greater than one might expect from the change of subject and sequence of thought.

Verses 1-2 celebrated the unique majesty of the One who came to possess his holy dwelling place. The Lord created all the world; therefore, he was not merely Israel's sovereign but ruled everyone who lived on the earth that he made. The psalmist wrote of earth or land as a foundation, the usual way that the Old Testament writers described it. The reference to seas and rivers probably was an allusion to Genesis 1:9-10 where the writer stated that waters were gathered together and dry land appeared.

The psalmist felt that the universal God should not be approached lightly and that even the place that symbolized his presence should be guarded carefully. Verses 3-6 raised an appropriate question: Who could be a guest of the most high God? The verses stated the moral conditions that were required for access to the Lord's presence and contended that God's holiness corresponded to his majesty. Both in substance and form, Psalm 15 is parallel to verses 3-6.

The third section (vv. 7-10) pictured the worshipers as they came to the entrance which was depicted as a fortress with doors through which one had to pass. The psalmist pictured the procession as it halted before the citadel and addressed the doors with a summons to open high and wide so that their King could enter. God was presented in two aspects: narrow and universal. As one mighty in battle, the Lord was thought of as Israel's God. As the commander of the hosts (a figure that often was used for the heavenly bodies), God was presented as universal in nature. Even in the midst of a seemingly nationalistic Psalm, the psalmist made a missionary emphasis: The Lord was the God of all the world.

The God of Steadfast Love (103:1-22)

Psalm 103 was designed to be used in public worship, not by a choir or a congregation, but by an individual. The deep spiritual expressions of personal piety move in a religious atmosphere closely akin to the New Testament spirit. The psalmist wrote the song after some experience of God's mercy in his life. His pouring out his heart in thanksgiving for grace and compassion suggests that the danger threatened his life and, at first, was looked on as a sign of God's displeasure. However, when the Lord acted to end the judgment, the psalmist expressed his gratitude and praise. The psalmist wrote to elevate his own soul and to fill those who heard with cheer. These facts have combined to make the song a favorite vehicle of praise for all ages. The words that were used expressed well the soul's feeling in view of God's redeeming love, mercy, and tender compassion for his people.

Verses 1-5 serve as a prelude in which with trustful gladness the psalmist sought to stir up his gratitude. He reviewed God's mercies to him and exhorted himself to praise God for the Lord's kindnesses. He wrote in the singular and created a solemn atmosphere by repeating the same opening phrase. He faced God's holiness with respect; at the same time, he gave himself over to the divine mercy that God's saving deeds revealed to him. From this inner action, both sentiments were woven into a marvelous melody. God dealt with the psalmist's sin and sickness, and the Lord brought inner vitality through his redeeming grace.

Verses 6-10 illustrated God's merciful dealings with examples from Israel's history. The psalmist related his experiences to his nation's past and realized that God works with persons and with nations. This fact was reflected in the covenant concept. Divine leadership of a nation was based on the commitment of the persons who made up the group. Israel's history was a proof of God's grace. God's patience with the nation's sins and failures showed clearly his slow-to-wrath attitude toward the poet and his people.

In verses 11-14, the psalmist continued his assurance of God's forgiving love in word pictures of exquisite beauty. He testified that even the largest dimensions of space could not reveal the difference between human sin and divine grace which God extended to sinners. He reinforced the truth with an illustration from family life to express God's concern for those who remained faithful to him.

In verses 15-18, the psalmist picked up and enlarged on a thought from verse 14. People die because they are finite, but God's mercy never fails. These thoughts were expressed in familiar phrases which contrasted the brief span of people's lives with the eternal nature of God's redeeming love.

The final section (vv. 19-22) stressed the Lord's universal sovereignty and called on the whole universe to unite in pledging allegiance to him. The psalmist contended that the whole human race should acknowledge the Lord's rule. He even called on the angels and the heavenly hosts to heed God's word and to do the things that the Lord commanded. The Psalm ended as it began, with a command to "bless the Lord"—but with one difference. At the beginning, the psalmist spoke to himself; but as he concluded, his heart went out in concern, compassion, and challenge to the whole world.

The God Who Keeps (121:1-8)

The Lord Gives Strength (vv. 1-2)

Pilgrims who encouraged one another as they marched to Jerusalem sang Psalm 121. Although the precise manner in which it was sung cannot be determined, the people probably chanted antiphonally as they marched. However, the reader may see development both in content and vividness as the march progressed. In verses 1-2, the pilgrims (or an individual) voiced calm trust in the Lord's help.

Originally, the psalmist wrote from a lonely place. The "hills" were not the "mountains of Israel" of which Ezekiel often spoke, but the mountain range on which Zion was built. Jerusalem was surrounded almost completely by mountains, and the plural may indicate the various ones or may be a majestic way of referring to the one where God's house was built. The psalmist felt that he was in need of great help and realized earthly assistance was not enough. He looked to the holy mountain even as people in all ages have looked for divine help when crises have come.

Although earlier translations render the first verse's second line as a statement, most scholars today interpret it as a question. Perhaps the psalmist knew the answer; thus, the question was rhetorical (expected no response) and provided the setting for the answer in verse 3. The words suggest a condition where danger threatened but no aid was evident. From a troubled and anxious mind, a plaintive plea was made.

As the procession marched, the reply came either from the soloist who asked the question or from the group in concert. Only one answer could be given to the anxious question. Israel's God differed from the heathen deities. The universe's great Creator was in sharp contrast to the impotent gods which were no gods. Verse 2 stated the basic truth that help comes from the Lord; the statement was made with such firmness and precision of thought that no one could escape the profound message it conveyed. Knowledge that help came from only one source which was available to every faithful Israelite provided firm ground for the hesitant persons. Complete trust in God would be a firm base for assurance as the psalmist sent the traveler on his way to worship.

Verse 2b literally reads: the one making heaven and earth. This vivid form suggests continuity of creative activity; it implies or even assures that God has power to help his people. This phrase is found often in the Psalms and contrasts God's power with the weakness that marked the heathen gods. The answer gives depth to the thought implied by the question. The Lord realizes that his people have needs, so he is near and ready to provide resources for them.

The Lord Protects (vv. 3-4)

The psalmist thought of the hazards that the imminent journey entailed and became specific as he outlined God's keeping

111

power. Some scholars have felt that in verses 3-4, the psalmist addressed himself. Others have contended that these verses contain the voice of another speaker who was encouraging the one who spoke first. In verse 3, the Hebrew literally reads: He will not abandon thy foot to the tottering. This was a comforting assurance for those who walked on the rocky plateaus as they plodded toward Jerusalem.

The psalmist believed that the Creator's activity extended beyond his (God's) original work; God refused to be dormant but continued to act because he is forever the *living* God. The contrast between the last phrase in verse 3 and verse 4 suggested the twofold thrust of the psalmist's conviction and outlook. History included both the individual and the corporate community to which one belonged. Both were important, and God was concerned for both. The psalmist passed from his own need to a general truth. He recognized that he could not find ultimate safety unless the nation was secure. He knew that Israel's Watchman exceeded in both interest and ability any human sentinel. A human watchman was liable to be overcome and could fail to maintain vigilance in protecting those to whom he was assigned. God would not fail his people; he never would be found "asleep at his post." The Lord would not—will not—"fall down on his job."

The Lord Defends (vv. 5-6)

Beginning with verses 5-6, the psalmist's confidence grew as he enlarged on the certainties that he expressed in verses 2-4. Those who spoke in this section and in verses 7-8 probably were the priests who were thrilled with the reality of God's protection. The psalmist reverently used the phrase "the Lord" twice, as he gave assurance concerning God's ability and willingness to work for his worshipers. The concrete picture language that was used to portray special blessings created a feeling of absolute security and gave enduring comfort and genuine promise.

The Hebrew word translated **shade** meant *shadow, protection, or defense.* The psalmist alluded to the "right hand" because that was the protector's place. Thus, the Lord would be ready to intervene and defend the person who needed to be guarded against approaching danger.

Verse 6 elaborated on the previous figure of speech. The word translated **smite** meant *to strike as with a rod or staff or with a plague or pestilence.* From this came the idea of *to kill* or *to*

112

slay. In the context of Psalm 121, the psalmist alluded to what today is called a sunstroke—the sometimes fatal effect of the sun on a person's vital organs. He was confident that God would protect his people from nature's perils as well as from people who sought the Israelites' destruction.

The psalmist also recognized the danger that often came during the night. The moon always has ruled the night and the sun has ruled the day. Thus, some interpreters have suggested that the reference to the moon in verse 6 referred to the sudden cold which follows intense heat in Oriental countries.

One of the most common ideas was that the moon made one become a lunatic. This old belief that the moon had the power to derange human reason has persisted through the centuries. The modern word comes through the Latin and means literally "moonstruck." For many years, Palestinians thought that sunstroke was caused by the demon that was active at midday and that intermittent-fever and lunacy came from the night demon. In the New Testament, the epileptic boy (Matt. 17:15) is described by a Greek word that literally meant *moonstruck*.

Probably, the psalmist had in mind the sudden changes from intense heat in the day to bitter cold at night and attributed these effects to the moon.

Today, how grateful we are for people who are trained in the medical field. When we have needs in this area, we want the most qualified person available to render the service. One minister has a prayer for the sick that goes like this:

> Father, we thank you for the skills of the physician
> and nurses, and we ask you to be with them as they
> minister to this patient. Yet, we also thank you
> that beyond all of our human wisdom and ability, we
> know that you stand within the shadow and keep watch
> above your own.

What a wonderful combination! We can have the best available medical care, plus a God who is present to care for his people.

The Lord Preserves (vv. 7-8)

In verses 7-8, the psalmist enlarged his thought still further by his assurance that God's protecting hand extended to him through all kinds of danger. He advanced his thought from the previous verses in which he pointed out specific evils and stated that God would be the people's protector in every peril which might arise. The word **evil** (v. 7) came from a term which

113

meant *to break* or *to break into pieces.* From this came the idea of something being hurtful to a person. The addition of the word "all" stressed the fullness of God's protective power. The psalmist knew that although life exposed people to a great variety of mishaps, no problem was beyond God's sheltering care.

The word translated **life** (often rendered soul) came from a term that meant *to take breath* or *to refresh oneself.* The noun meant *breath* or *anything that breathed,* such as an animal or a person. From this came the idea of soul as the principle of life or life itself. The Hebrews thought of a person in terms of a being rather than to fragment the various parts of one's nature. The human being was more than soul, spirit, flesh, or heart. A person was a total being who was responsible for his/her free choices. In this sense, the translation *life* in the context of Psalm 121 was excellent.

In verse 8, the words "going out and . . . coming in" suggested not only one's departure from his home and back but also dangers incurred in travel, especially pilgrimages. From the time that one set out on the journey to its completion, God was there to assure a safe return. Also, the phrase could have meant all of a person's pursuits in daily living. The solemn closing phrase "from this time forth and for evermore" opened up a wide area of thought. The phrase literally meant: from hence forth even unto the age. Thus, the words embraced not only creation and history but also eternity. Psalm 121 closed with a strong statement that reflected implicit faith in God. The song has become a source of comfort to countless people who have sought assurance and help in their struggles.

The God Who Is Always There (139:1-24)

God's All Knowledge (vv. 1-6)

The psalmist knew that an unexamined life was not worth living, but he also was convinced that human analysis was not enough. He went beyond finite scrutiny into the sphere where God investigates and evaluates. The word translated **searched** (v. 1) meant *to analyze accurately* or *thoroughly.* In the Hebrew text, the word "known" did not have the pronoun **me** attached as a suffix, but most students have felt that it was implied. The

Psalm's outward form revealed the psalmist's attitude; it showed the interaction of awe and wonder at God's greatness combined with trustful and devoted submission to him.

In verse 2, the pronoun "thou" was emphasized. The words stressed that God's all-seeing scrutiny made certain nothing would be hidden from him (God). One could not change locations to escape God's observation and evaluation. By the words translated "when I sit down" and "when I rise up," the psalmist could have meant that God noticed him in the two extremes of his life: when he was depressed and when he was prosperous. Or, he could have meant that whether he rested or was active, God saw him—his whole life.

The word translated **discernest** (v. 2) meant *to understand,* or *to be intelligent or wise.* The word stressed God's unique ability to penetrate into the psalmist's mind and to see what he wished to do. The term "afar off" suggested not merely that the thought was far off but that the Lord was removed from the psalmist's physical presence.

In verse 3, the Hebrew word translated "searchest" meant *to spread, scatter, disperse, or winnow.* The idea was that of the farmer casting seed loosely about as the wind blows dust and then to winnow by throwing grain into the wind. The chaff was blown away, and the part that was saved was valuable. The psalmist meant that God sifted him and removed all that was valueless. He contrasted his walking with the time that he was resting. On both occasions, God knew all about him. The word **acquainted** meant that God was thoroughly familiar with the psalmist.

Verse 4 expressed the psalmist's astonishment when he realized that God not only knew his words in advance but knew what they meant. He no longer belonged to himself because invisible bonds connected him to God. In verse 5, the word translated **beset** meant *to bind up, beseige, press upon, or compress.* The term referred to the seige of a city, of troops pressing on in war. From this came the idea of hemming in or closely surrounding so that no way of escape remained. Verse 5 began a transition from the idea of God's knowing everything to his being present everywhere.

In verse 6, the psalmist faced the disturbing fact that because of God's supreme knowledge, he (the psalmist) only could express his wonder and confess that he could not grasp God's fullness. His exclamation of awe was the logical conclusion of his prior statements. The word translated **wonderful** meant *to be extraordinary, great,* or *marvelous.* God's fullness was too great for the psalmist to comprehend.

The word translated "high" (v. 6) implied something that could not be reached. The word **attain** came from a term that meant *to do anything, prevail,* or *overcome.* The psalmist recognized that God surpassed all human comprehension.

God's All Presence (139:7-12)

In verses 7-12, the psalmist did not write as a sinner with a bad conscience; rather, he reflected the innate reaction of a man who trembles at God's greatness. He realized that escape from God would be impossible even if he (the psalmist) desired it. The phrase "thy Spirit" (v. 7) has been called the "living energy of a personal God."[1] The phrase "thy presence" could be rendered literally: from thy face. Poetically, the term suggested the One who filled the universe and manifested his relationship with his created beings.

Verse 8 contained two "for instances" concerning attempts to escape God's presence. If the psalmist had been able to go up to heaven, God would have been there. The word rendered "heaven" is plural and includes everything above the earth—the highest world.

The Hebrew word translated **make my bed** (v. 8) came from a term which meant *to spread down* or *strew.* The word **Sheol** comes from a verb which means *to ask, inquire of, interrogate.* The noun derived from this word means *grave* or *abode of the dead.* The Israelites of that day did not have the full revelation of Jesus Christ. They did not understand the mystery behind the grave as the Savior's resurrection later made clear. The latter part of verse 8 literally reads: there thou. The two possibilities that the psalmist suggested pointed to the extremities known in that day: as high as one could go or as deep as one could go.

Verse 9 presented another supposable case. The "wings" suggested swiftness and referred to the rapidity with which the morning seems to fly. The psalmist did not know the exact velocity of light, but to him its flight was the most rapid of anything that he knew. The word rendered **morning** came from a term which meant *to break, to break forth.* From this came the idea of the morning or daybreak, the Aurora—the first approach of the morning light. Actually, these beams were no swifter than others; but they seemed to be because they penetrated the darkness so quickly.

The verb **dwell** (v. 9) meant *to abide or settle down*. The phrase **uttermost parts** came from a word which means *to stay behind or tarry*. From this came the idea of behind or after. To the Hebrews, the hinder side or back part was the west. Of course, the psalmist had in mind that the Mediterranean Sea was west of Palestine. Thus, he made a poetical contrast between the east where the sun rises and the west where it sets.

The psalmist added a thought to that of verse 8, stating that God's protecting power and providential care, rather than merely his presence, would accompany him in any eventuality (v. 10). Some interpreters have held that the psalmist meant he could not escape God's authority and control.

Translators vary in rendering the first phrase in verse 11. Probably, the best translation is: If I say, Surely the darkness will cover me. The verb **cover** means *to fall on one unexpectedly*. In the context of Psalm 139, the phrase meant that though darkness came suddenly to overcome the psalmist, the attempt would be futile because God would make the darkness light.

The psalmist contended that to hide from God under the cover of darkness was as useless as to attempt to escape from him by moving from one place to another. The light of God's presence would banish the terrors of darkness. The psalmist did not refer so much to his confidence in God's protection as he did to his conviction of God's knowledge.

Verse 12 declared that the distinction between day and night had no conditioning influence on God who is superior to all created things and is light in himself. The psalmist knew that darkness did not serve as a magic cloak to make its wearer invisible but was penetrated easily by God's glance, though human eyes could not pierce it.

The last phrase in verse 12 literally reads: As is the darkness, so is the light. It summarizes in precise fashion the thesis in the two verses. Though the psalmist did not spiritualize, one should remember that disappointments, sorrows, troubles, cares, and losses—often regarded as darkness—may be conquered through God's light.

Martin Luther, like the psalmist, often had periods of discouragement and depression. At one such time, he saw his wife dressed in mourning. Surprised, he asked who had died. "Do you not know?" she replied; "God in heaven is dead." "How can you talk such nonsense, Katie?" Luther said. "How can God die? Why, He is immortal, and will live through all eternity." "Is that really true?" she asked. "Of course," Luther said, "how can you doubt it?" "And yet," she said, "though you do not doubt that, yet you are so hopeless and discouraged." Then, Luther said, he observed what a wise woman his wife was.

God's Works (vv. 13-18)

When the psalmist failed to escape from God, he adopted the opposite course and turned to him in a quiet, personal way through creation. He came closer to God as he meditated on the creative process that brought his life into being. He reasoned that God must know him perfectly because the Lord ordered the start of his life and foresaw all the future. In verse 13, the word "thou" was made emphatic. The Hebrew term translated **didst form** meant *to found* or *create*. God created the psalmist's life, and only God had such power.

The psalmist would have agreed that God owns his creation; however, the thought that he expressed in verse 13 was that from the beginning, God set him upright or stood him up. The word translated **inward parts** meant the reins or kidneys—the location of the secret workings and affections of the soul. As the heart was thought to be the seat of a person's intelligence, the kidneys were viewed as the center of one's emotional life.

The word translated **knit . . . together** means *to weave or interweave*. God had put the psalmist's parts together as a weaver or a basket maker.

The psalmist's change of attitude caused him to express himself in a hymn that interrupted his train of thought and took the form of a testimony. In verse 14, the word **praise** meant *to confess openly and freely*, to confess or celebrate publicly one's feelings. One cannot be dogmatic concerning whether the psalmist wrote about God or God's creation as "fearful and wonderful" (v. 14). The word **fearful** came from a term that meant *to produce awe* or *reverence*, while the term **wonderful** came from a word which meant *to distinguish or separate*. God or his creation produced awe because he and what he did belonged in a special, distinct category.

Whether the psalmist wrote about God or thought about his own bodily formation as he became acquainted with his anatomy, his words aptly described his thoughts. Beyond doubt, he indicated God's creative activity with the phrase "thy works" as he felt excitement, wonder, and admiration—even with his limited knowledge of the human body. In the Hebrew text, the statement, "Thou knowest me," literally reads: My soul is knowing. The psalmist referred to his total person, not to an isolated part of his nature.

In verse 15, the psalmist thought about the period during which his body was taking shape, and he testified that God understood everything about its formation. The word **frame** came from a term which meant *to be or become strong or powerful.* The noun meant something strong—for instance, the bones (skeleton), body, or even self. The psalmist acknowledged that when others could not see him taking shape, God saw him clearly.

The phrase **intricately wrought** conveyed the idea *to deck with color or variegate.* The psalmist referred to the various and complicated tissues of the human frame—tendons, nerves, veins, arteries, and muscles—as though they had been woven together. He considered the womb as dark and mysterious. He meant that God's work took place in a dark, obscure area where no person's eye could see.

In verse 16, the first word in the Hebrew text means an undeveloped embryo. Later, the meaning became unformed matter or an unfinished vessel. The word came from a term which meant *to wrap or roll together.* Anything rolled or wrapped together or folded up would convey the idea, but especially appropriate is the fetus where the body's members have not assumed their distinct form and proportions.

Older Hebrew scholars understood the phrase "in thy book were written" (v. 16) to refer to the limbs which would develop from the embryo. Later, however, some scholars contended that the doctrine of predestination was reflected in the words. To them, the phrase "days that were formed for me" suggested that the psalmist meant the length of life which one would live was determined before the person was born.

The word **book** means *to number or recount,* or *to write by engraving,* as on a stone or a rock. The term **written** means *to describe in writing.* One cannot state dogmatically what the psalmist had in mind. The Hebrews saw everything as a direct result of God's work with no secondary causes considered. The psalmist stated truth that provided support and substance because it enabled him to see life as being under God's sovereignty. This gave him a real sense of security.

Once more, the words of Psalm 139 rang with ecstasy. In verse 17, God was presented as the loving, divine Thinker who was concerned for his creation. In the Hebrew text, the phrase "unto me" was placed first in the sentence. This indicated how important the psalmist was to God. The statement could be rendered literally: To me, how they are precious, thy words, God! The word translated **precious** meant *to be dear or esteemed.* Some scholars have felt that the word had the idea of being beyond the mind's grasp or overwhelming, and they have contended that the psalmist contrasted his knowledge of God with God's knowledge of him.

Some translators have rendered the phrase "how great is the sum of them" literally: How strong are the heads of them. The psalmist felt that to add up all of God's thoughts in his favor would be a task beyond human power. To him, each thought of God was beyond human reach, and the totality of them could not be measured.

In verse 18, the psalmist climaxed the section composed of verses 13-18 by comparing God's thoughts to the sands of the sea. His final statement pictured a person falling asleep counting God's blessings; yet, he was occupied with and contemplating the mystery of God's being. When the person was aroused, God was still there. Though the individual became lost in deep and profound meditation, God's eyes never closed. Some scholars have interpreted the words to indicate the resurrection, but this probably was not their original meaning. In the context of Psalm 139, the psalmist wrote about God's great goodness and praised God for his wonderful works. More truth followed later!

God's Enemies (vv. 19-22)

The psalmist turned from God's wonders in the universe to question how God could tolerate the existence of evil people who hated the Lord. He prayed that God would remove them from the earth. The abrupt transition and the words' vindictive spirit has presented a problem to many interpreters. Some have held that revelation is progressive and that the psalmist simply had not come to the New Testament concepts. Others have suggested that since the evil people were out of harmony with God's world, the psalmist felt that God should not tolerate their living contrary to the divine will. Some have suggested that God knew all things, including the evil persons' guilt; therefore, they were in great danger.

Verse 19 literally reads: if thou will slay the wicked. However, the words can be translated as an imperative that expresses the psalmist's desire. The following words indicate that he was asking God to destroy the evil people. The word "depart" clearly was imperative. The Hebrew word translated "blood" was plural, which indicated violent crimes. The psalmist felt that he could have no fellowship with such evildoers and that God also should banish them from his sight.

The first phrase in verse 20 could be rendered literally: who speak thee. The word which followed meant wickedness. The wicked people hid their evil schemes by piously using God's word. Some Hebrew scholars have suggested the translation *rebel against thee* as the true meaning of the phrase. The final phrase could be translated literally: Lifted up to vanity are thine enemies. Many translators insert the words "thy name" in order to parallel the previous phrase's meaning. God's foes used his name in vain; thus, they violated the Third Commandment. Translations vary, and one cannot be dogmatic about the actual words. However, the psalmist's desire and spirit have seemed clear. He wanted God to intervene against those who were opposing the Lord.

Some translators have rendered the opening word in verse 21 as "Look!" They believe that this captures the psalmist's impatience. The phrase "them that hate thee" conveys intense feeling. In the second phrase, the word **loathe** can be rendered *abhor* or *be grieved with*. It emphasizes intimate, personal feeling. In a sense, the term "loathe" explains the psalmist's meaning of "hate" in the previous line and somewhat softens the problem that one might have with his vindictive spirit. Since he was zealous for God and his cause, he was opposed to, and even at enmity with, those who rebelled against God.

In verse 22, the psalmist amplified his feelings. The word **perfect** came from a term that meant *to be complete or finished*. In the Hebrew text, it was placed first in the sentence; the word's position emphasized the depth of the psalmist's feelings. The last phrase in verse 22 could be rendered literally: foes they are to me. The psalmist felt duty bound to keep alive in his heart a burning indignation against moral evil, selfishness, untruth, and injustice.

A Final Prayer (vv. 23-24)

Aware of his limitations and vulnerability, the psalmist felt so inadequate that he asked God to examine him completely. He wanted God to search him thoroughly in order that any imperfections might be brought to light and corrected. He made clear that he had no spirit of presumptuous self-confidence but honestly wanted to be saved from self-deception.

The word **thoughts** (v. 23) probably means *disquieting thoughts*. The words "search" and "try" are similar in meaning. The psalmist probably used them for variety in style rather than with any shade of difference between them. The term **know** means *to preceive or be acquainted with*; it is used many times for the intimacy that is involved in the marriage relationship. The words stress the intense desire that God examine the secret citidel of life.

The psalmist drew a practical conclusion from his basic attitude to God that he expressed throughout Psalm 139. He knew that he could not bring any achievement of which he could boast and on which he could rely. He realized that God held the final decision, and he was willing to trust himself to the One who had all knowledge and all power. The phrase **wicked way** literally meant *a way of grief or pain*. The phrase **way everlasting** meant *the path of life* contrasted to the wicked way which led to destruction (Ps. 1:6).

How far the psalmist saw into the future life cannot be determined from the text. One possible translation could be: *the ancient way*. Those who have seen verse 24 against the background of the Lord's resurrection know that death does not interrupt the journey of the righteous person for a moment. Those who pray sincerely find their spiritual needs met through God's revelation in Jesus Christ.

Lessons for Life from Psalms 24; 103; 121; 139

Fellowship with God requires moral purity.—A secondhand suit in a clothing store had a sign on it: "Slightly soiled, reduced in value." Life is that way also. Moral impurity soils and reduces life. Believers' strength can be renewed and sustained, if their hearts are pure.

Because God is merciful, people can be forgiven.—The Bible sets a high standard of holiness that persons cannot reach. However, parallel to God's holiness is his mercy. In Jesus Christ, redeeming love at its greatest is revealed.

What God's people need, he wants to give.—Sometimes, believers think that something they want is so important that God should grant it immediately. However, he is more concerned about their character than their comfort. He knows when they need something, and his schedule for giving it is never wrong. Many times, he attempts to move his people to meet others' needs.

Although God is for his people and they should be for him, they still must allow him to decide when and how his enemies should be punished.—Believers' judgment is not always accurate; therefore, they must not be too hasty to condemn.

---

1. See A. F. Kirkpatrick, *The Book of Psalms* (New York: Cambridge Press, 1900), II:128.

Personal Learning Activities

1. Psalm 24 celebrated God as the _____.
   (Choose the proper answer from the list.)
   (1) Lord of Hosts   (3) Redeemer
   (2) Shepherd of Israel (4) King of Glory
2. In Psalm 103, the psalmist expressed his gratitude for God's _____. (Select the correct response from the list.)
   (1) Majesty   (3) Power
   (2) Holiness   (4) Steadfast love
3. Psalm 121 stressed the _____ of God's people. (Select the proper response from the list.)
   (1) Prosperity (3) Duties
   (2) Security   (4) Troubles
4. Psalm 139 celebrated God's (choose the correct answers from the list):
   ____(1) All knowledge ____(3) All presence
   ____(2) Creative power ____(4) Love

Answers: 1. (4); 2. (4); 3. (2); 4. (1), (2), (3).

8 Songs of Thanksgiving

The Hebrews felt that the greatest kind of prayer was to give gratitude for God's goodnesses. Indeed, the most attractive Hebrew hymns are the songs of personal thanksgiving.

The songs of gratitude became related vitally to the payment of vows, and they can be understood properly only in relation to such service. To the Israelites, a pledge represented something beyond the normal demands of religion. It was voluntary; it started within the individual's will. The Hebrews expressed gratitude and discharged obligations in the presence of the congregation. All eyes were fastened on the worshiper as he told the story of God's deliverance or of some other blessing. Many songs that began as private hymns of personal piety found their way to the religious ritual where they became widely known and loved.

The four songs in this study celebrate various blessings from God. Psalm 32 is a beautiful song of thanksgiving for God's forgiveness. Psalm 34 expresses gratitude for God's hearing the psalmist's cry for help. Psalm 92 gives thanks to God for some unnamed benefit which had been received. Psalm 116 states the psalmist's gratitude to God for delivering him from the dreaded Sheol—the place of departed spirits. These Psalms stress the deep emotion that only poetry or song can express adequately. They encourage people to hold fast to their faith in God during crises. All of these Psalms reinforce the truth that God hears and responds to sincere prayer.

Gratitude for God's Forgiveness (32:1-11)

The Joy of Forgiveness (vv. 1-2)

Psalm 32 showed a fervor which only could have been the fruit of personal experience as it described and celebrated the happiness of one who knew God's grace. Most scholars have seen this song as a parallel to Psalm 51. The latter described David's heartfelt cry of repentance because of his sin with Bathsheba; Psalm 32 recorded the glorious peace which came to one whose guilt had been removed.

David began with the term "blessed," the same word that was used in Psalm 1 to describe the ecstatic delight of one who follows God's commands. Psalm 32 expressed the view that one who was restored to fellowship with God after a grievous sin felt the same delight as the one who served God faithfully. Since other Scriptures teach that all persons sin, Psalm 32 made an even greater claim on the human heart. Like azure arising behind the storm cloud, forgiveness became the victor's wreath which God presented to one who had conquered pride and surrendered in repentance to him.

David used the same three words for wrongdoing—*transgression, sin,* and *iniquity*—that appear in Psalm 51, but the terms that he employed for removing the effects are different. The term **forgiven** came from a word which meant *to lift up, carry, or carry away.* From this came the idea of bearing the guilt for one, forgiving, or pardoning. The word **covered** literally meant *to conceal in order that a thing would no longer come into view.* The offender would be regarded as one who had not sinned.

In verse 2, the word **impute** means *counting, regarding, or reckoning something to someone.* The psalmist wrote about one whom God did not charge with guilt or whom God treated as though he had no guilt. The word "deceit" referred to the matter being discussed—the phrase which taught that the one condition which was essential above all others for forgiveness was absolute sincerity. Only those who were sincere and honest in confessing their sins could be sure that their sins were forgiven. David looked back on his own experience and realized that only his candor had paved the way for him to be restored to fellowship with God. He did not mean that one must be sinless; rather, he meant that a person must be truthful with God and one's self. Divine grace, and human sincerity without deceit, formed the two foundation pillars of uninterrupted fellowship with God.

The Misery of Unforgiven Sin (vv. 3-4)

David looked back on his previous condition when glumly he had kept silent. He remembered how at first, he had stilled his conscience's voice which warned him about the sin that he had committed. Serious physical and mental problems came because he had disharmony within his soul. Though he was reconciled and healed, he remembered the inner misery of his lacerated heart. He poured out the inner struggle through which he went before he obtained remission of sin. He felt God's chastening hand heavy on him.

Remorse caused an actual sickness. No doubt, David suffered and complained but did not pray. Thus, no relief came because he would not confess his sin. Probably, about a year transpired between the time when Nathan the prophet confronted David with the king's sin and when David poured out his heart in repentance and acknowledged his wrongdoing.

The word translated **declared not** (v. 3) comes from a term which has the idea *to be dumb, silent, or deaf.* The form of the word in verse 3 means *to keep silent or quiet.* The word trans-

lated **wasted away** literally means *to grow old* and thus *to deteriorate or wear out*. The term **groaning** comes from a word which means *to roar* (as a lion) or *to thunder*. As long as David stayed silent about his sin, his life declined.

In verse 4, the phrase "day and night" indicated that David suffered all the time; he had no relief. His burden was constant, and he could not go on bearing it. His troubled conscience allowed him no peace of mind. The weight of unforgiven sin pressed down so strongly that he felt great pressure. However, he had the insight to perceive that his suffering came because he had rebelled against God's standards of holiness and purity. Later, he saw that his misery was part of the healing process. He came to realize that his distress which came because he was outside God's will actually was God's mercy driving him to a place of repentance. He discovered that to be chastised because of sin was better than to be left to sin's progressive ruin.

The word **strength** (v. 4) comes from a term which literally means *moisture or vital power*. David experienced a drying up of his energies and compared it to a drought which caused all things to become desolate. A burning fever consumed him as his life withered. His mind's distress because of long-continued conviction produced a fevered soul that affected his body like physical illness. A musical rest which indicated a pause in the music followed this verse.

The Way to Salvation (v. 5)

In the Hebrew text, in the first phrase of verse 5, the words "my sin" and "my iniquity" appear before the terms "acknowledge" and "did not hide." Such a structure stresses the words which express David's wrong. The form of the word "acknowledge" suggests the start of a process of confessing his sin to God. Repentance is the first step of a lifelong attitude of turning from sin. Actually, David did not give information to God but admitted to himself that he had sinned. The word translated "did . . . hide" emphasizes the word "not": David did *not* hide his wrong. He brought up the festering sense of guilt from his subconscious into his conscious mind.

The turning point came when David decided to be honest and forsake the acting that he had been doing. The word "guilt" more often was translated *iniquity*, but in the context of verse 5 it indicated moral crookedness *and* the blame that went along with it. David realized that his mind would be relieved only when he admitted to God and to himself that his sin was his problem. He also learned that complete peace could come only when he openly confessed the awfulness of it.

Exhortation to Others (v. 6)

David was happy because he had experienced God's grace, and he wanted to share his happiness with others. He stated a formula that he knew would work because he had seen it operate. He learned that people who would not confess all of their sins to God only tortured themselves until they cast their burdens on the One who could and would forgive. The word **godly** came from the beautiful, often-used term that meant *kindness, graciousness,* or *mercy.* One never should forget that those who were conscious of God also possessed great compassion for others.

The phrase **at a time of distress** (v. 6) literally means *in a time of finding.* David did not mean that God would be gracious only at set times or that God would be disposed more strongly to show mercy at one time than another. Rather, without delay people should come to him in repentance.

David used a bold figure to express his confidence that had come because God had pardoned him. Calamity and judgment would not overwhelm him, for he came to God in sincerity. He assured those who prayed to the Lord that they would be like one who stood on a high rock, safe from the waves that dashed against it below.

Application to Self (v. 7)

David imagined the threatening flood of life's experiences as he addressed the Lord. He knew that the assurance which he had promised to others could be his also.

In verse 7, David changed the figure; but the meaning remained. He alluded to concealment from an enemy. The word translated **trouble** came from a term that meant *to tie or bind up.* A further meaning was *to be hostile to.* From this came the words *adversary* or *enemy.* David knew that he was safe in God's presence because the Lord's deliverance surrounded him like a bulwark. He rejoiced because he was set free from the agony of sin and no longer was afraid no matter what the future held for him.

Counsel to Sinners (vv. 8-9)

David referred to his experience as qualifying him to advise others. He had learned much from his painful experience and felt fitted to impart valuable knowledge to those who asked how they could be delivered. Verse 8 began the second part of Psalm 32; this section used a form of exhortation that was designed to teach and was phrased in a much more restrained fashion. David used the same style as the Wisdom writers did with terse, pointed sayings; and he tried to make his message clear by using parables and proverbs.

The expression **with my eye upon you** (v. 8) means *watch over* or *keep an eye on* to prevent the person from making a mistake or taking a wrong turn in the path. Most interpreters who accept David as the speaker in verse 8 suggest that he fulfilled the promise which he made in 51:13 to "teach transgressors . . . [God's] ways."

The words **instruct** and **teach** (v. 8) are similar but have slightly different meanings. The first word means *to cause to consider, to give insight.* The second term means *to throw or shoot,* then *to point out, show.* In verse 8, the term means *to direct.*

Verse 9 used another bold figure of speech to warn people not to resist God's will or to neglect instruction. The "horse" was used to illustrate a person who by nature is wild and unwilling to be caught and made obedient. The "mule" was noted for its stubborn nature. The phrase "without understanding" applied to both animals.

David knew that a person became a subject of God's government by cheerful, willing submission, not by force. People were not brought into or kept in God's service by coercion. They had to yield themselves willingly by submitting to God's guidance and direction, and they were to be controlled by reason and conscience. People were not brutes; they had a higher nature and were to allow themselves to be governed by it.

The Happiness of Trusting (vv. 10-11)

Psalm 32 ended with a general statement and appeal. Verse 10 confirmed the warning that was given in verse 9 by contrasting the state of the ungodly to the state of the faithful. The word rendered **pangs** came from a term which meant *to be in pain or grieved.* One who persisted in self-will and hardness of heart in relation to God faced pain and grief. No doubt, David referred to his own suffering which arose from his remorse. all who followed the way of the wicked also would suffer the same misery.

The phrase **steadfast love** translates the Hebrew term *hesedh*, a word that David and other writers used so often. This term of compassion and affection has no exact counterpart in English; it refers to God's mercy and love that is available to all people.

The final verse made clear that through faith, David had become a testimony to God's grace. He stated clearly that one should not allow joy in the heart to remain unexpressed. The language of song was/is one of the most effective ways to give God credit for his grace. The Psalm's beginning and ending harmonized in a mighty symphony of people's delight in God. Those who followed David's example and confessed their sins found that God was not slow to pardon; he filled their lives with peace and put praise on their lips.

Gratitude for Answered Prayer (34:1-22)

The psalmist had passed through a crisis from which God had delivered him. In his song, he recast his personal experience into valid truths. He adopted the style that the writers of Wisdom Literature employed. This was especially true from verse 11 onward. Psalm 34 followed the pattern of Psalm 25; each verse began with a successive letter of the Hebrew alphabet. One slight variation existed in verse 6 where the second phrase continued the style. A supplementary verse concluded the song and compensated for verse 6 with two parts of the acrostic which brought the sum to twenty-two verses—the total letters in the Hebrew alphabet.

The title attributes the Psalm to David. The occasion that is given—when David pretended to be mad before Abimelech—is described in 1 Samuel 21:11-15. The seeming discrepancy between Achish and Abimelech in the historical account is explained best by considering the latter to be a title, not a proper name, similar to the Egyptian title Pharaoh.

The main thrust of Psalm 34 is to present a reason for a person to trust God during crises, leading to a life that validly can consider God to be Protector and Friend. The song contains four essential parts. All are related to the main thrust, but they suggest different trains of thought.

Verses 1-6 praised God for past deliverance. Praise was combined with an exhortation for others to join the celebration. David made clear that the help he experienced from the Lord was not limited. Others could enjoy the same benefits, especially those who were afflicted, forsaken, crushed, and made desolate by their needs.

Verses 7-10 are a general summary that came out of David's experience. The verses celebrate the privileges which come from confiding in God. Included also is an exhortation for others to commit themselves without reserve to God who is ready to meet their needs and to make possible their enjoying an abundant life.

Verses 11-14 gave an urgent invitation to the young people and called on them to trust the Lord and to follow God's teachings. David wrote out of experience; he recalled his former life and presented it as an invaluable lesson. The passage's tone seemed to suggest that David was growing old but still remembered vividly earlier events that had shaped his life.

The final section (vv. 15-22) summarized David's attitude toward God's protecting power. The righteous people were safe in the Lord's hands and could rely on him even though they faced suffering. David also stated that those who opposed God and his people faced punishment. He closed with an assurance that God's mercy hovered around those who were committed to him, and no one who sincerely sought the Lord's protection would be disappointed.

Gratitude for God's Love and Faithfulness (92:1-15)

The psalmist considered praise to the Lord to be a duty and a delight. Jewish tradition considered Psalm 92 to be ancient; the Targum title read: "A Psalm of praise and song which the first man uttered up: on the day of the Sabbath." However, no evidence supported this claim. But Judaism early began to use Psalm 92 in public worship on the sabbath when it was recited to music as a hymn of thanksgiving.

The main thrust of Psalm 92 dealt with individual thanksgiving. The psalmist lived in a world where those who did evil flourished, and this raised a problem for the righteous people as they sought to praise God for his goodness.

The sabbath was an ideal time for one to meditate on Psalm 92. On this day, one's spiritual nature was heightened as spiritual perception became clearer. One could view trying situations with a better outlook as the passing nature of the material things and the permanence of the spiritual realm came to mind—especially during worship.

Verses 1-4 affirmed the value of thanking God and celebrating his name. The regularity of the Lord's mercies and actions deserved special consideration from people who had known such blessings. The psalmist testified that God's activities had brought him happiness. His words called for an outburst of musical praise.

Verses 5-9 mentioned God's activities and indicated their scope and intensity. Brutish people who were sensuous and who could not grasp spiritual things could not appreciate divine truths. Such people did not see that those who did evil had passed away quickly. Animal instincts overruled their spiritual impulses, and their destiny was only misery. They had lapsed into deceptive illusion and faced total ruin. However, the Lord would remain while his foes perished and were scattered.

Verses 10-15 discuss the prosperity and security that the righteous enjoy. God's favor is extended to them in contrast to his punishing those who do evil. Religion's influence plays a major part, for God extends his goodness to people who honor him. He prepares them to be useful and cheerful through the passing years. The righteous people's prosperity ("flourish like the palm tree," v. 12) and length of life ("grow like a cedar in Lebanon," v. 12) are a contrast to the state of those who oppose God's ways. Psalm 92 closes by affirming God's strength which he uses for his people.

Gratitude for Recovery (116:1-19)

An Expression of Gratitude (vv. 1-2)

The psalmist began Psalm 116 with heartfelt praise to God for answered prayer. He still felt the thrill that came when God graciously heard him and met his needs. A literal reading of verse 1 could be stated: I love because God hears. The object of the psalmist's love was not given, as though the full heart had no need to identify the One whom it praised. The form of the word translated "has heard" expressed a repeated or continuous action. More than one answer to prayer had been received. The God who had heard would continue to hear when one of his people prayed.

The Hebrew text has no conjunction between "voice" and "supplication," which suggests that the phrase should be translated: the voice of my supplication. No doubt, in his time of trouble the psalmist spoke audibly as he asked God to hear him.

In verse 2, the word "because" repeats a motive which some interpreters feel is unworthy of true worship. The main reason for loving God should be his excellent nature, but other reasons surface. Few people are capable of an entirely unselfish love. Many worshipers give their devotion and loyalty to the Lord because of benefits he has given them which have awakened love and gratitude.

The word translated **inclined** (v. 2) meant *to bow down*. The expression **as long as I live** literally meant *in my days*. The psalmist had a firm faith that God answered prayer: he was determined to show his practical belief by regular worship habits. He knew that God had answered in the past, and he had faith that God would not change.

A Description of Deliverance (vv. 3-4)

With Oriental vividness, the psalmist told how his calamity had begun to bind him with its fatal power. In verse 3, the word translated "encompassed" was first in the sentence and thus was emphasized. The psalmist was surrounded by evil; he was hemmed in, and no way of escape seemed open.

The word **snares** (v. 3) means *to writhe, to be in pain*, or *to travail as a woman in labor*. The noun is used for the throes of childbirth, writhing, or pains in general. The term **pangs** means *distress* or *adversity*. The word "distress" is formed on the same basic Hebrew term. The word translated **anguish** means *grief* or *sorrow*. It comes from a term which means *to be pained in mind, to be sad*. Note that the verse describes the psalmist's condition with the terms pains, adversity, distress, and grief. The terms describe a life reduced to its lowest point.

In verse 4, the expression "name of the Lord" was emphasized. The psalmist called on God because of the Lord's revealed character, not merely his name. He sought deliverance from death, not spiritual salvation—though that may have been included. The psalmist had his back to the wall, and the Lord was his only hope. He knew that he was in peril, so he pleaded for the Lord's mercy. In Hebrew, the word **life** is the term often translated *soul*; it means the totality of being, not merely a fragment of one's nature.

A Portrait of God (5-11)

The psalmist had experienced a threefold deliverance: (1) from imminent death to life; (2) from sorrow to joy; and (3) from insecurity to stability. Stirred to the depths, his soul thrilled as he told the story to his fellow worshipers. In verse 5, he used two different Hebrew words to express the Lord's kindness and compassion. The first word, translated **gracious,** came from a term that meant *to be compassionate.* The second word, rendered **merciful,** came from a term that meant *to love tenderly, to pity.*

The psalmist added the term "righteous" between the two words for God's kindness to stress God's justice in the midst of his compassion. He knew that people had no claim to God's favor; but because the Lord loves, he will take the first step to set things right and to restore broken fellowship between him and his people.

The word translated **simple** (v. 6) means *open, easily persuaded or enticed.* The word is not related to one's intellectual ability; rather, it refers to being influenced or led astray easily. This word also can mean one who is open to good influences as well as bad ones. However, in the context of verse 5 the psalmist meant those who needed instruction and discipline; and he was convinced that God constantly guards those who are weak and easily influenced.

The word translated **brought low** (v. 6) originally meant *to hang down* or *to be languid, weak, and feeble.* The word rendered **saved** meant *to deliver or set free.* The form of the word in verse 6 indicated repeated acts of deliverance. God had delivered the psalmist more than once; when he had arrived at low points in his life, God had helped him up.

Although verses 5-11 were a monologue concerning God, the psalmist addressed himself with encouraging words as he remembered God's mercy. He urged himself to let go of anxiety and resume the peace that sprang from confidence in God.

The word "rest" (v. 7) was plural, which suggested intensity or full and complete security. The term translated "dealt bountifully" came from a term which meant *to give, do, or show*, either in a good or a bad way. From this came the idea of *to repay or recompense*. In the context of verse 7, the psalmist encouraged his soul to have perfect peace because God had worked for him in his dire need. Therefore, he had every reason to believe that God would continue on his behalf.

Once more, in a direct dialogue and in an intimate way, the psalmist felt compelled to confess directly to God what he owed the Lord. He used language which indicated that he had been dangerously ill. The word translated "soul" in verse 8 was the same term that was rendered "life" in verse 4. The Hebrews did not draw fine distinctions between different parts of one's personality. The tears that the psalmist mentioned probaby were those which he shed during his sickness and fear of dying. The word "stumbling" indicated that he had been unable to pursue his life's journey. Taken collectively, the entire context seemed to indicate strongly one occasion: a time of dangerous illness.

In verse 9, the form of the verb "walk" could have had a future thrust, although the psalmist did not anticipate his future actions until the section that began with verse 12. Whether the thrust was present or future, he wrote of free and joyous service to God in contrast to the paralysis of existence in the grave which he had dreaded.

The first part of verse 10 has been translated: I believed, therefore, have I spoken. The Hebrew would permit this translation. Paul picked up this thought to express his confidence in the gospel and his boldness to declare its truth because he believed so strongly in it (2 Cor. 4:13). The next phrase in the Psalm, however, suggested that the psalmist meant his faith held firm during the time his distress was acute.

In verse 11, the word "consternation" translates the Hebrew term best. The Hebrew word means *to be alarmed*. The psalmist meant that he spoke out of fear and excitement, not as the result of reflection. In his great peril, he spoke in an agitated state of mind. Whether his statement was true or false was not the question. Calm reflection might confirm his impression, but he had jumped to conclusions and had spoken without considering his words.

A Promise for Service (vv. 12-19)

Overwhelmed by God's favor, the psalmist faced his responsibility with integrity. He knew that those who had been blessed were obligated to give themselves in service. His question was more than rhetorical. He recognized that human aid which was delusive and undependable had not brought him through his struggles. He realized that he must return adequate dedication for a love and mercy so great and so undeserved. By the word "bounty," he attempted to express the scope of God's mercies to him. God's love constrained the psalmist to show his gratitude by his deeds.

Verse 13 alluded to the drink offering which the psalmist planned to bring when he came to the Temple. The figure came from pouring out libations as a sacrifice to the Lord and drinking a portion as a part of the thanksgiving service. The psalmist planned to do this as a symbol of God's great, manifold deliverance. The word translated "lift up" was the same one that often was used for forgiveness, since the word also implied lifting up and carrying away. Some versions have the word "take," but in the context of verse 13, "lift up" probably expressed best

the meaning. Of course, the psalmist would give God the honor; he would "call upon the name of the Lord" to let everyone know that he attributed his healing to God's gracious hand.

The "vows" to which the psalmist referred in verse 14 were the solemn promises that he made during his sickness. Although he made them in private, he planned to perform them in public. For some reason, he turned to the thought of death and stated that God regarded his loved ones' deaths as important and even valuable. The psalmist meant the death of a good person was so important that God would not allow it to take place except in times and circumstances that would fulfill his purposes. The psalmist must have reasoned further that God had more for him to do and thus spared him to bring honor to the divine name.

The word "precious" (v. 15) came from a term which meant *to be dear, esteemed, or prized*. The term referred to precious stones because they were costly and valuable. The psalmist reasoned that though a godly person's death could bring glory to God, one's life could honor him even more.

Verse 16 follows logically the reasoning of the statement in verse 15. The psalmist recognized that he must live as one who had been redeemed, for he was living proof of the Lord's favor and mercy. His humble self-description expressed feelings of dependence on God for the future as he had relied on the Lord in the past. He thanked God for a good heritage; he referred to his mother as God's instrument to bring him into the world and to surround him with godly influences. His family background was a part of his redemption.

The "sacrifice of thanksgiving" to which the psalmist referred in verse 17 was detailed in Leviticus 7:11-15. He wanted to express publicly his gratitude for all that the Lord had done. In verse 18, he repeated his intent to make his thanksgiving known to all the people. The phrase "courts of the house of the Lord" referred to the place where the Israelites assembled, not to the outer Court of the Gentiles. Only the priests could enter the holy precincts of the Temple, and only the high priest could enter the holy of holies.

The concluding statement, "praise the Lord," consists of two Hebrew words, *hallal* and *yahweh*. Put together, the two form the English word *hallelujah* which is used in poetry and prose today. The psalmist's song begins with a testimony of love and concludes with an outburst of praise!

Lessons for Life from Psalms 32; 34; 92; 116

Guilt is a heavy load to bear.—After a young lady confessed a moral indiscretion, she said to her pastor: "I feel that everyone who looks at me can tell by my face what I have done." The pastor assured her that her countenance did not reveal her wrong. After prayer in which they asked God's forgiveness for her wrongdoing, she left the pastor's office a new person. The weight of sin had been lifted.

Only God's grace can deal adequately with people's problem of guilt for wrong that they have done. Only God's mercy can work healing at the depth where people hurt because of unforgiven sin. Confession to God that is specific and pointed is necessary. Such confession is answered by a compassion that frees a person as nothing else can do.

Young people can profit from the experience of older persons.—The old cliche, "Rome wasn't built in a day," applies to a life also. Experience can be a great teacher.

God answers the prayers of his people. He answers them in his own time and in his own way, and sometimes his answer is no. But God hears the pleas of those who trust him and who depend on him, and he gives what is best.

To oppose God is to invite disaster.—To set oneself against God's purpose is to face ultimate judgment. People can exclude themselves from God's grace, and their lives will be lived in vain and will come to nothing.

Redeemed people should serve.—Believers will have to live a lot more like their Redeemer before many lost persons will trust Christ. The best way for believers to live like Jesus is to dedicate themselves to serve in his name. He left the glory of heaven for the troubles of earth. Christians, too, must be concerned for people's needs in order to find happiness and lead nonbelievers to faith in Christ.

God's gifts to us call for our daily gratitude. The gifts of life, strength, purpose, and people who care about us should draw our repeated expressions of thanks to God. In like manner, God's working on our behalf in crises should draw our gratitude for One who brings to bear his grace and power for us.

Personal Learning Activities

1. Psalm 32 expressed gratitude for _____. (Choose the correct answer from the list.)
   - (1) Life
   - (2) Health
   - (3) Forgiveness
   - (4) Prosperity

2. Psalm 34 gave thanks for (select the proper response from the list):
   - ____(1) Deliverance from crisis
   - ____(2) God's creation
   - ____(3) Military victory
   - ____(4) A good harvest

3. Psalm 92 contended that God's people enjoyed prosperity and God's favor. True____ False____

4. Psalm 116 celebrated deliverance from _____. (Choose the proper answer from the list.)
   - (1) Wrong
   - (2) Enemies
   - (3) Death
   - (4) Ignorance

5. In Psalm 116, the psalmist promised to pay his tithes in response to God's goodness. True____ False____

6. In Psalm 116, the psalmist wanted to express his thanksgiving _____. (Select the correct answer from the list.)
   - (1) Privately
   - (2) Briefly
   - (3) Publicly
   - (4) Silently

Answers: 1. (3); 2. (1); 3. True; 4. (3); 5. False; 6. (3).

The Church Study Course

The Church Study Course consists of a variety of short-term credit courses for adults and youth and noncredit foundational units for children and preschoolers. The materials are for use in addition to the study and training curriculums made available to the churches on an ongoing basis.

Study courses and foundational units are organized into a system that is promoted by the Sunday School Board, 127 Ninth Avenue, North, Nashville, Tennessee 37234; by the Woman's Missionary Union, 600 North Twentieth Street, Birmingham, Alabama 35203; by the Brotherhood Commission, 1548 Popular Avenue, Memphis, Tennessee 38104; and by the respective departments of the state conventions affiliated with the Southern Baptist Convention.

Study course materials are flexible enough to be adapted to the needs of any Baptist church. The resources are published in several different formats—textbooks of various sizes, workbooks, and kits. Each item contains a brief explanation of the Church Study Course and information on requesting credit. Additional information and interpretation are available from the participating agencies.

Types of Study and Credit

Adults and youth can earn study course credit through individual or group study. Teachers of courses or of foundational units also are eligible to receive credit.

    1. Class Experience.—Group involvement with course material for the designated number of hours for the particular

course and reading the textbook. A person who is absent from one or more sessions must complete the "Personal Learning Activities" or other requirements for the course.

2 Individual Study.—This includes reading, viewing, or listening to course material and completing the specified requirements for the course.

3. Lesson Course Study.—Parallel use of designated study course material during the study of selected units in Church Program Organization periodical curriculum units. Guidance for this means of credit is in the selected periodical.

4. Institutional Study.—Parallel use of designated study course material during regular courses at educational institutions, including Seminary Extension Department courses. Guidance for this means of credit is provided by the teacher.

Credit is awarded for the successful completion of a course of study. This credit is granted by the Church Study Course Awards Office, 127 Ninth Avenue, North, Nashville, Tennessee 37234, for the participating agencies. Form 725 (available free) is recommended for use in requesting credit.

A permanent record of courses and diplomas will be maintained by the Awards Office. Twice each year, up-to-date reports called "transcripts" will be sent to churches to distribute to members who participate in the Church Study Course. Each transcript will list courses and diplomas that participants have completed and will show progress toward diplomas that are being sought. The transcript will show which courses are needed to complete diploma requirements. A diploma will be issued automatically when the final requirement is met.

Detailed information about the Church Study Course system of credits, diplomas, and record keeping is available from the participating agencies. Study course materials, supplementary teaching or learning aids, and forms for record keeping may be ordered from Baptist Book Stores.

The Church Study Course Curriculum

Credit is granted on those courses listed in the current copy of the *Church Services* and *Materials Catalog* and the *Church Study Course Catalog*. When selecting courses or foundational units, check the current catalogs to determine what study course materials are valid.

How to Request Credit for This Course

This book is designed for a course in the subject area Bible Studies.

This course is designed for 5 hours of group study. Credit is awarded for satisfactory class experience with the study material for the minimum number of hours which includes reading the textbook. A person who is absent from one or more sessions must complete the "Personal Learning Activities" or other requirements for the materials missed.

Credit also is allowed for use of this material in individual study and in institutional study, if so designated.

The following requirements must be met for credit in this course:

1. Read the book *Psalms: Songs from Life.*
2. Attend at least 5 hours of class study or complete all "Personal Learning Activities" (see end of each chapter). A class member who is absent from one or more class sessions must complete "Personal Learning Activities" on chapters missed. In such a case, he or she must turn in his/her paper by the date the teacher sets, usually within ten days following the last class.

Credit in this course may be earned through individual study. The requirements for such credit are:

1. Read the book.
2. Complete the "Personal Learning Activities" on the chapters.

Credit in this course may be earned through study in an educational institution, if so designated by a teacher. The requirements are:

1. Read the book.
2. Fulfill the requirements of the course taught at the institution.

After the course is completed, the teacher, the study course records librarian, the learner, or any person designated by the church should complete Form 725 ("Church Study Course Enrollment/Credit Request") and send it to the Awards Office, 127 Ninth Avenue, North, Nashville, Tennessee 37234. In the back of this book the reader will find a form which he may cut out, fill in, and send to the Awards Office.

CHURCH STUDY COURSE
ENROLLMENT/CREDIT REQUEST (FORM-725)

PERSONAL CSC NUMBER (If Known)

INSTRUCTIONS:
1. Please PRINT or TYPE.
2. COURSE CREDIT REQUEST— Requirements must be met. Use exact title.
3. ENROLLMENT IN DIPLOMA PLANS— Enter selected diploma title to enroll.
4. For additional information see the Church Study Course Catalog.
5. Duplicate additional forms as needed. Free forms are available from the Awards Office and State Conventions.

TYPE OF REQUEST: (Check all that apply)

- ☐ Course Credit
- ☐ Enrollment in Diploma Plan

- ☐ Address Change
- ☐ Name Change
- ☐ Church Change

DATE OF BIRTH ⬆

Month	Day	Year

REQUEST FOR

☐ Mr. ☐ Miss
☐ Mrs.

Name (First, Mi, Last)

Street, Route, or P.O. Box

City, State, Zip Code

CHURCH

Church Name

Mailing Address

City, State, Zip Code

COURSE CREDIT REQUEST

Course No.	Use exact title
04098	1. Psalms: Songs from Life
Course No.	Use exact title
	2.
Course No.	Use exact title
	3.
Course No.	Use exact title
	4.
Course No.	Use exact title
	5.

ENROLLMENT IN DIPLOMA PLANS

If you have not previously indicated a diploma(s) you wish to earn, or you are beginning work on a new one(s), select and enter the diploma title from the current Church Study Course Catalog. Select one that relates to your leadership responsibility or interest. When all requirements have been met, the diploma will be automatically mailed to your church. No charge will be made for enrollment or diplomas.

⬆

Title of diploma	Age group or area
1.	
Title of diploma	Age group or area
2.	

Signature of Pastor, Teacher, or Study Leader	Date

MAIL THIS REQUEST TO ⬅

CHURCH STUDY COURSE AWARDS OFFICE
RESEARCH SERVICES DEPARTMENT
127 NINTH AVENUE, NORTH
NASHVILLE, TENNESSEE 37234

FORM-725 (Rev. 7-83)

Kelly Johnson, 1-939-1250 phone
Taught at 44 Ave. Baptist Church
Jan 13, 14-16, 20   1985
        Students attending

1. Hockett, Ken —————— lll
2.   "   , Marianna llll
3. STARK; Gene   llll
4   "   Nadine llll
5 MEEK; Don   llll
6   "   Marlena lll
⑦ SMITH; Dillon llll
⑧   "   Helen llll
9 KERLIN; Lew   l
10   "   Bev   ll
11 MOORE, Marilyn-1
      (Bill out sick)
12. Pearl ULLRICH_llll
13. MOORE; Betty - llll
14. ULLRICH, Stan - llll
⑮ RENFRO, Jim llll
16 BARTLETT; Irene llll
17. WILDE, Jacquie lll

18 BERDAHL, Rob...
19 BOSMA, Evelyn
20. SANDERS, Mar...
21. JOHNSON, Louis...
22, Janet Hockett
23. THOMPSON, Jim
24.   "   Sue
25 BARNES, Lon
26 " Kathy A...